SUPER SUNDAY

SUPER SUNDAY

THE OFFICIAL PHOTOGRAPHIC CELEBRATION OF THE SUPER BOWL

NAL BOOKS

NEW AMERICAN LIBRARY

TIMES MIRROR

NEW YORK AND SCARBOROUGH, ONTARIO

A National Football League Book

Copyright 1983 by National Football
League Properties, Inc. All rights reserved.
No part of this book may be reproduced
or transmitted in any form or by any means,
electronic or mechanical, including
photocopying, recording, or by any information
storage and retrieval system, without permission in
writing from the publisher.

Prepared by National Football League
Properties, Inc., Creative Services Division.

Library of Congress Cataloging in Publication Data
Main entry under title:
Super Sunday.

    ''A National Football League book.''
    1. Super Bowl Game (Football)—History.
I. Didinger, Ray. II. National Football League
Properties, inc. Creative Services Division.
GV956.2.S8S94   1983   796.332'7   83-11482
ISBN 0-453-00441-5

NAL BOOKS TRADEMARK REG. U.S. PAT. OFF.
AND FOREIGN COUNTRIES
REGISTERED TRADEMARK—MARCA REGISTRADA
HECHO EN CRAWFORDSVILLE, INDIANA

SIGNET, SIGNET CLASSICS, MENTOR, PLUME, MERIDIAN,
and NAL BOOKS are published in the United States by The New
American Library, Inc., 1633 Broadway, New York, New York
10019; in Canada by The New American Library of Canada Limited,
81 Mack Avenue, Scarborough, Ontario M1L 1M8.

First Printing, July, 1983

1 2 3 4 5 6 7 8 9

PRINTED IN THE UNITED STATES OF AMERICA.

contents

Introduction   17
   by Ray Didinger

Games   33

Players and Coaches   83

Sidelines 117

Emotions 137

Appendix 172

Captions and Credits 190

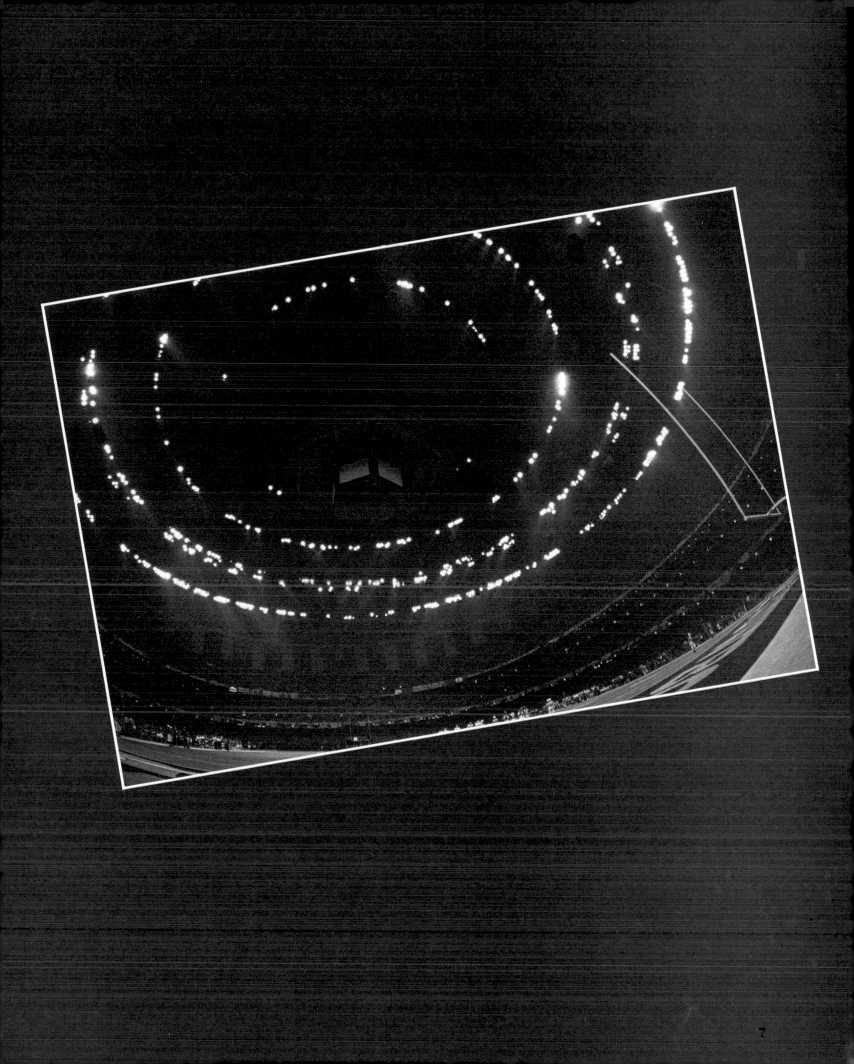

SUPER BOWL XII

SUPER BOWL VII

SUPER BOWL XVI

First World
Championship
Game AFL vs NFL

SUPER BOWL

SUPER BOWL XVII

SUPER BOWL XI

SUPER BOWL V

SUPER BOWL XV

SUPER BOWL IV

SUPER BOWL IX

SUPER BOWL II

SUPER BOWL VIII

SUPER BOWL XIV

SUPER BOWL III

SUPER BOWL X

SUPERBOWL VI

Introduction

by Ray Didinger

"If Jesus were alive today, He would be at the Super Bowl."

Norman Vincent Peale

Super Bowl. The Skylab 3 astronauts watched it from outer space in 1974. Former President Gerald Ford watched it from Jerusalem in 1979. A mother in San Jose, California, couldn't get anybody to attend her baby's baptism because of it in 1975.

"What did she expect?" the family said. "She knew the game was on."

Super Bowl. It is the reason Georgetown University Hospital installed television sets in the labor rooms of the maternity ward. Before that, fathers-to-be often delayed bringing their wives to the hospital until the game—and, in some cases, the postgame show—had ended.

Super Bowl. *Time* Magazine calls it the Great American Time Out. Work ceases, romances cool, even crime disappears. The day the Chiefs played in Super Bowl IV, the Kansas City police had just one burglary and they waited until halftime to interrogate the suspect. He asked the first question:

"What's the score?"

Super Bowl. When the Redskins and Dolphins met in January, 1983, the television audience was 110 million. That's enough people to fill every one of America's movie theaters 15 times over. That's more people than live in most countries. It is the late Marshall McLuhan's global village come to life, and all because of a football game.

Actually, the Super Bowl is more an event than a game, more a spectacle than a contest. It has become the sports altar of modern society, the place where young men reach for footballs and catch immortality instead. The Greeks found their gods on Mount Olympus; we find ours tumbling into the end zone in New Orleans, Pasadena, and Miami.

Broadway Joe Namath, Vince Lombardi, Lynn Swann. They are legends because they never lost a Super Bowl. Bud Grant and Fran Tarkenton are legends because they never won one. There are no small successes in Super Bowls, nor are there any little failures. Kick the winning field goal and you get a call from the Oval Office. Miss a block at the goal line and you wind up on "Face the Nation."

Super Bowl is Americana at its best and worst. It is loud and overdressed and self-important, yet it is also human and honest and passionate in a way that touches us all. It assaults our sensibilities, like a marching band coming through our living room. Yet there is something about it, something unique and dynamic, that draws us back in ever-increasing numbers.

"The Super Bowl," NFL Commissioner Pete Rozelle once said, "is like the last chapter of a hair-raising mystery. No one would think of missing it."

Super Bowl is more than a mere mystery, of course. It is drama and comedy. It is an unheralded San Francisco defense making its stand at the one-foot line against Cincinnati. It is Miami kicker Garo Yepremian ("No one believes me, but I have a very good arm") watching the football squirt from his grasp and turn into a Washington touchdown.

Super Bowl is vindication. It is Jim Plunkett escaping from oblivion to quarterback the Oakland Raiders past Philadelphia. Super Bowl is frustration. It is Bob Lilly firing his silver helmet at the Goodyear blimp as the Dallas Cowboys lost to Baltimore in the final seconds.

Super Bowl is blood 'n' guts. It is Jack Youngblood playing on a broken leg. It is Dwight White busting out of the pneumonia ward to face the Vikings. It is Al Atkinson telling the New York Jets trainer to hurry up and tape his separated shoulder so he can start the second half.

Super Bowl is hearts 'n' flowers. It is most valuable player Fred Biletnikoff standing on the interview platform with his arm draped around his son. It is Joe Greene handing the game ball to white-haired owner Art Rooney and saying, "This is for you, Chief." It is Joe and Cass Montana leaving the Silverdome hand-in-hand, like two kids on a Hallmark card.

Super Bowl is style. It is Vince Ferragamo's Hollywood smile; it is Jack Lambert's Transylvania scowl. It is Joe Namath's sideburns; it is Johnny Unitas's crewcut. It is John Madden jackknifing on the sidelines; it is Tom Landry, arms folded, impassive, like a commuter waiting for the 5:07 to Saddlebrook.

Super Bowl is the macho swagger of Joe Kapp; it is the balletic grace of Lynn Swann. It is the icy silence of Duane Thomas; it is the disc jockey chatter of Joe Theismann. It is Terry Bradshaw quoting Willie Nelson; it is Calvin Hill quoting Keats. It is All-American boys; it is placekickers in wooden shoes. It is Rhodes Scholars and street fighters.

Super Bowl is Rocky Bleier and his Purple Heart; it is Carl Eller and his Purple People. Super Bowl is nicknames and No-Names. It is Doomsday versus Orange Crush; it is Hogs versus Killer Bees. It is Hacksaw and the Mad Stork; it is Snake and Lenny the Cool. It is Butch and Sundance riding off, unbeaten, into the sunset.

Super Bowl is for kids such as Jim O'Brien who are too young to feel the pressure; it is for warhorses such as Max McGee who are too old to worry about it. Super Bowl is where the dynasties, Green Bay and Miami, come to secure their place in history. It is where the Steelers and Eagles come to bury the past.

Super Bowl is for the people. It is Pittsburgh fans weaving through the French Quarter at 4 A.M. chanting "Dee-fense." It is Terrible Towels and white hankies and cheerleaders with Bengal-striped faces. It is limousines and Lear jets and yachts. It is school buses and campers and Valley girls with their thumbs pointed toward Pasadena.

Super Bowl is Madison Avenue and it is Middle America. It is Big Business and it is Small Towns. Super Bowl is Jack Kent Cooke in his houndstooth hat brandishing the Lombardi Trophy. It is the Green Bay bartender taping Nitschke's photo over the cash register and saying, "Drinks on the house." The moment belongs to everyone.

Super Bowl is hype and hope, elation and disappointment. It is June Taylor and Jim Taylor; it is America's Teams and the American Dream. It is Butch Johnson's impossible catch; it is Jackie Smith's impossible drop. It is Fred Williamson saying, ''We're gonna whip Green Bay's ass....'' It is Roger Staubach saying the Lord's Prayer.

Super Bowl is all of that and more. It clears our streets and fills our family rooms and pulls us together like moon walks and Royal Weddings have yet to do. Even when it came at the end of the tattered, strike-torn season, the Super Bowl had us on our feet, cheering and forgiving all the Sundays that dawned so empty.

Super Bowl is ritual and it is legend. It is the toy we never outgrew, it is the dame we will never leave behind. Let the sociologists argue about the symbolism of it all. Let your mother-in-law worry about the pot roast. When it's fourth-and-goal and Bradshaw's asking for quiet and I'm leaning forward in my chair hollering, ''Give it to Franco,'' I know I'm where I'm supposed to be.

In the beginning, there were no Roman numerals affixed to the Super Bowl. In fact, there was no such thing as Super Bowl. Not formally, at least.

When the Green Bay Packers and the Kansas City Chiefs met in the Los Angeles Coliseum on January 15, 1967, it was officially called ''The AFL-NFL World Championship Game.''

The title certainly covered the essentials. This was, indeed, the first summit meeting of the two professional football leagues following the merger agreement in 1966. The name was clear and to the point, but it lacked, well, pizzazz.

The club owners wanted something catchy for the marquee. ''The Big One'' was voted down. Too sophomoric. ''The Final Game'' was also rejected. Too ominous. It sounded like the world was going to end in the fourth quarter.

Then Lamar Hunt, the Kansas City owner, remembered the Silly Putty ball his daughter played with around the house. What was it she called it, her Super Ball? Yeah, that's it. Super Ball...Super Bowl...hey, that's not bad.

The title was there in January, 1967, but no one pushed it too hard because, frankly, no one knew what to expect when the NFL and AFL champions met for the first time. What if it wasn't super? Hunt's title was soft-peddled by the media, at least at first.

The mood surrounding the Green Bay-Kansas City game was one of curiosity more than passion. For seven years, the old, established NFL and the fledgling AFL had fought for college players, fans, television time, and newspaper space, but never had they fought it out where it counts—on the field.

This game would bring the best of the rival leagues together, with 50 million TV viewers and everything on the line. The two teams were so different, their philosophies so contrasting, it was impossible to get a handle on what might happen.

The traditionalists said the Packers would win easily, because of their big edge in experience and coaching. Kansas City supporters pointed out the Chiefs' advantage in size and speed, not to mention their slick, multi-set offense orchestrated by head coach Hank Stram.

According to the Green Bay players, Lombardi was a nervous wreck in the days leading up to the first Super Bowl. ''Vince was a man possessed,'' said tackle Bob Skoronski.

The Packers had won four NFL titles in six years. They had established themselves as one of the truly great teams in the league's history. All that did, Lombardi felt, was make winning the Super Bowl even more imperative.

Game I   **Green Bay Packers**

"Vince was really hooked on this thing about carrying the flag for the NFL," said guard Fuzzy Thurston. "Before we left for Los Angeles, he called us together and told us this was gonna be the biggest game we had ever played.

"Vince told us we were representing the whole league, we couldn't let our peers down. He read us a few telegrams. I remember one was from George Halas, another was from Wellington Mara. They all said pretty much the same thing: 'Go out there and show those [AFL] clowns who's boss.' "

"We were confident, but Vince made sure we weren't overconfident," said full-back Jim Taylor. "We studied the Kansas City films and Vince kept pointing out individuals. He'd say, 'See that tackle [Buck] Buchanan? He's a good one. See that linebacker [Bobby] Bell? Watch the play he makes here.'

"Vince respected the Chiefs, therefore, we HAD to respect the Chiefs. He told us to forget the point spread [the Packers were 14-point favorites] and get our heads into the game. He said we had worked hard to get where we were, but we could blow it all by losing to Kansas City."

Meanwhile, in the Kansas City camp, cornerback Fred Williamson was telling newsmen how his forearm blow to the head—"the Hammer," he called it—would dismember the Green Bay receivers. It was all a put-on, of course, but no matter. Williamson became Super Bowl's first media darling. It's no coincidence he wound up in Hollywood two years later.

There were a few ragged edges to the big event, one involving television coverage. CBS was the NFL network, NBC was the AFL network, and both claimed broadcast rights to the title game. Commissioner Rozelle allowed the two networks to air the contest simultaneously, with the Los Angeles area blacked out.

Then there was the question of which football would be used. After much deliberation, it was decided the NFL ball would be used when the Packers were on offense, the more-tapered AFL ball when the Chiefs were on offense.

Local interest in the game was less than overwhelming. The tickets, priced at $12, $8, and $6, were a tough sell. On a warm, sunny California day, the first AFL-NFL title game drew 61,946, less than two-thirds capacity at the Los Angeles Coliseum. Scalpers wound up selling $8 tickets for $2 apiece.

As kickoff approached, however, the enormity of the event settled over the participants. Frank Gifford recalls interviewing Lombardi prior to the game. "During the five minutes or so we talked," Gifford said, "he held onto me and he was shaking like a leaf. It was incredible."

Emotions were running even higher on the Kansas City side.

"We were scared to death," linebacker E.J. Holub admitted later. "We had the feeling we were going to go out there and the Packers were going to tear our heads off. Guys in the tunnel were throwing up and wetting their pants."

The only one who had his pulse rate in check was the 34-year-old McGee, Green Bay's reserve split end. McGee, who spent the week sneaking out of the Packers' Santa Barbara quarters and sampling the Los Angeles night life, was totally confident.

McGee had played sparingly during the regular season, catching only four passes, but when Boyd Dowler, who came to the game with a bad back, was injured on the first series against the Chiefs, Max took over.

"I didn't have much left," McGee said, "but there was one play I could still run and that was the quick slant. Bart knew it, so he audibled to it once we got into Kansas City territory.

"I got inside [Willie] Mitchell, but Bart threw the ball behind me. I reached back

Game II   **Green Bay Packers**

Game III   **New York Jets**

to knock it away; I wanted to make sure Mitchell didn't intercept. I couldn't believe it, but the damn thing stuck in my hand. I held it there for a second, then I squeezed it against my hip.

"I turned upfield, Mitchell dove for me and missed and I had a clear road to the end zone. It was only thirty-seven yards, but it seemed a lot longer. I didn't know if my legs would hold up."

They did and Max McGee scored the first Super Bowl touchdown. He scored on another one-handed catch in the third quarter, a 13-yard reception from Starr. McGee finished with seven catches for 138 yards as the Packers rolled over the Chiefs 35-10.

After the game, newsmen pressed Lombardi for a comparison between the Chiefs and the teams he faced in the NFL. "Kansas City has a good team," Lombardi said, "but it doesn't compare with some of the teams in the NFL. Dallas is a better team. That's what you want me to say, isn't it? There. I've said it."

It was much the same story the next year when the Packers met the AFL champion Oakland Raiders in Super Bowl II in Miami's Orange Bowl.

The Packers won 33-14 and it might have been a routine exercise if it were not for the fact it was Lombardi's farewell as head coach in Green Bay. Two days before the game, Lombardi confirmed the rumors to his players. "This may be the last time we're all together," he said.

"We all had lumps in our throats," Starr said.

The Packers dedicated the game to Lombardi—"the old man," they called him—and they played accordingly. The Raiders never had a chance. As the final seconds ran off the clock, guard Jerry Kramer and tackle Forrest Gregg hoisted Lombardi onto their shoulders.

"One more time, coach," Kramer said.

Lombardi smiled. "This is the best way to leave a football field," he said.

If you are looking for a demarcation point, a point where the Super Bowl left the realm of a mere football game and became cosmic theater, you can set the time machine for January 12, 1969.

The place was Miami's Orange Bowl. The event was Super Bowl III, the Baltimore Colts versus the New York Jets. This was the one quarterback Joe Namath guaranteed, the one that unfolded like a Harlequin paperback, the one that was played out against a backdrop of Ft. Lauderdale nightclubs and squealing chorus girls.

If the first two Super Bowls reflected the personality of Lombardi—grim, uptight, monastic—then Super Bowl III reflected the personality of Namath—loose, hip, and irreverent. Lombardi saw the Super Bowl as a sacred mission. Namath? He did his pregame interviews at poolside while a blonde rubbed suntan lotion on his back.

Broadway Joe brought star quality to the Super Bowl. Sure, the game was big, but Namath was bigger. He picked up a new first name that week: Brash. As in, "Brash Namath says five AFL quarterbacks better than Earl Morrall. . ."

The Jets were 17-point underdogs. Namath heard the odds and laughed. "I didn't know we were that bad a team," he said.

The Colts had finished the season 13-1 and they crushed Cleveland 34-0 in the NFL title game. "In the opinion of many," wrote William N. Wallace in the *New York Times,* "the Baltimore Colts are the best team in the history of professional football."

"The opinion of many what?" Namath asked.

On the Sunday night before the game, Namath met Baltimore's Lou Michaels in a Ft. Lauderdale bar and told him, "We're gonna kick the hell out of your team." Four days later, Namath went before the Miami Touchdown Club and announced, "We are

Game IV   **Kansas City Chiefs**

going to win Sunday, I guarantee you.''

The Baltimore players taped the quote to their lockers and bathroom mirrors. Namath was unmoved. ''If they need newspaper clippings to get up for a game,'' he said, ''they're in a helluva lot of trouble.''

If the Colts had any qualms about the game, they increased in the first quarter. Lou Michaels shanked a 27-yard field goal attempt to waste an early scoring opportunity. A few minutes later, middle linebacker Al Atkinson tipped a Morrall pass to cornerback Randy Beverly in the end zone, killing another Baltimore drive.

On the Colts' bench, heads dropped, shoulders sagged. The mood for the afternoon was established.

In the second quarter, Namath took over. He guided the Jets downfield, dissecting the Baltimore defense, the NFL's best, with the skill of a surgeon. He hit split end George Sauer, Jr., for a first down at the Baltimore 23. Runs by Emerson Boozer and Matt Snell punched it down to the 4.

''The Colts were cursing themselves in their huddle,'' New York center John Schmitt recalled. ''They were mad as hell that we were moving on them.''

Again, Namath handed off to Snell. The 6-foot 2-inch, 220-pound fullback slanted off the left side, picked up blocks by tackle Winston Hill and guard Bob Talamini and dove into the end zone. Snell's touchdown, followed by Jim Turner's conversion, gave the AFL its first ever Super Bowl lead, 7-0.

With 30 seconds left in the half, the Colts had a chance to tie. They ran a flea flicker with Morrall handing off to Tom Matte, then Matte lateraling back to Morrall. Jimmy Orr was all alone in the end zone, waving like a shipwreck victim flagging down a rescue plane, but Morrall never saw him.

Instead, Morrall threw down the middle for Jerry Hill. The ball hung up and safety Jim Hudson intercepted.

''We were losing our poise,'' Morrall said, ''and our self-assurance was draining away, little by little, like beans trickling out the bottom of a torn sack. It was sad.''

In the third quarter, Baltimore's head coach Don Shula sent in the old master, Johnny Unitas, to see if he could get the Colts going. Unitas gave it his best shot, driving Baltimore to its only touchdown. But three field goals by Turner and Snell's tough running (30 carries, 121 yards) put the game away for New York, 16-7.

Broadway Joe had pulled off the biggest upset in pro football history. He had completed 17 of 28 passes and earned the most valuable player award. What's more, he wiped out all the jokes about his ''Mickey Mouse league.'' He brought credibility to the AFL, and to the whole notion of the Super Bowl.

''We made history today,'' Namath announced in the locker room. For once, no one called him brash.

Lest anyone thought the New York Jets' victory was a freak occurence, the Kansas City Chiefs came along the next year and made it two in a row for the AFL. The Chiefs dominated the Minnesota Vikings 23-7 in Super Bowl IV, played in Tulane Stadium, New Orleans. Once again the central character was the quarterback of the AFL champions, but this time the story line was different. For Namath, Super Bowl week was all laughs and good times. For the Chiefs' Lenny Dawson, it was loneliness and personal torment.

Four days before the game, NBC news reported a U.S. Justice Department Task Force was launching a ''major gambling investigation'' and it planned to subpoena seven pro football players to testify regarding their relationships with ''underworld figures.'' Dawson was one of those players.

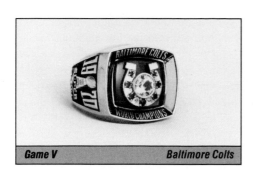

Game V   Baltimore Colts

Game VI   Dallas Cowboys

Meanwhile, Dawson locked himself in his room and refused to accept any calls. The siege of Lenny the Cool had begun.

That was impossible, of course. The gambling reports dominated Super Bowl week. Every day, newsmen wrote about Dawson "performing under a cloud of suspicion." The pressure became so intense, Jackie Dawson, Len's wife, kept their two children home from school because she was afraid of what the other kids might say.

Johnny Robinson, the all-pro safety, was Dawson's roommate. He spent the week assuring the media that Lenny was holding up well under the strain. "If there's anybody who can handle this situation," Robinson said, "it's Len Dawson."

Privately, however, Robinson expressed concern. "Lenny said he's never been through anything like it," Robinson told friends. "I know it hit him real hard. It ate him up inside. It looked to me as if he aged five years from Tuesday to Thursday."

Just before the Chiefs took the field on Super Sunday, the telephone rang outside the locker room. The equipment manager answered and called for Stram.

"Hank Stram of the Kansas City Chiefs?" the operator asked.

"That's right," Stram said.

"Hold one second, please, for the White House."

At first, Stram throught it was a prank. He was about to hang up when he recognized President Richard Nixon's voice at the other end of the line.

"Coach," President Nixon said, "I know there is nothing to the rumors that your team was involved in early in the week. I just wanted to tell your players, and Lenny Dawson in particular, to dismiss those rumors from their minds and go out there and play like champions."

Stram thanked the President for his good wishes, then he led his team out to meet the Vikings.

The Chiefs controlled the first half, with Dawson calmly picking apart the Vikings' defense. A short pass here, a draw play there, with an occasional end-around just to keep things interesting.

"Look at that," Stram said, pointing at the befuddled Minnesota secondary. "It looks like a Chinese fire drill out there."

Jan Stenerud kicked three field goals to give Kansas City a 9-0 lead, then Minnesota's Charlie West fumbled a kickoff return at his own 19. Five plays later, running back Mike Garrett scored standing up and the Chiefs were rolling, 16-0.

The Vikings, led by their fiery quarterback Joe Kapp, rallied with a touchdown in the third quarter and the Minnesota fans came to life for the first time on the cold, dreary afternoon. But, moments later, Dawson and Otis Taylor combined on a 46-yard touchdown pass and the momentum swung back to Kansas City.

Dawson finished with 12 completions in 17 attempts and he was named the game's most valuable player. Nixon called back to extend his personal congratulations. It was a six minute call, which, with the weekend rate, cost the taxpayers $2.68.

Later, a newsman asked Dawson the obvious question: Did he feel he was "vindicated" by his performance?

"I don't look at it in that vein," Dawson said softly. "Unfortunately, it put a great deal of stress and strain on me, and more so on my family, but I asked the Good Lord to give me the strength and the courage to play my best, and asked Him to let the sun shine on my teammates today."

In the weeks that followed, the gambling story faded. The Justice Department probe never made it to the Grand Jury. Pete Rozelle formally cleared Len Dawson's name. Life went on.

Game VII   **Miami Dolphins**

It is interesting to note the Chiefs' victory started a trend that continued for the next three years, a trend that saw past Super Bowl losers return to the big game and walk away with the championship.

In Super Bowl V, the Colts returned to the Orange Bowl and defeated Dallas 16-13 as rookie Jim O'Brien kicked the decisive field goal with nine seconds left. It was a fitting ending to a bizarre afternoon that included 10 turnovers, 14 penalties, and a touchdown pass that skipped off three sets of hands.

Wrote Dick Young in the *New York Daily News*: "I don't know if I just witnessed the greatest football game ever played, or the worst."

Super Bowl VI will be remembered as the day the Cowboys finally proved they could win The Big One. Tired of being labeled "next year's champions" and "chokers," the Cowboys put on an awesome display of power, crushing the Miami Dolphins 24-3 in New Orleans. Roger Staubach threw two touchdown passes and was named most valuable player.

"I never saw a Cowboy team so intense, so ready to play," said tackle Bob Lilly. "And it had nothing to do with money. We would have paid the league for the chance to play in that game, that's how much we wanted it."

The next year, it was the Dolphins' turn to come back, but when they did, they set a precedent all their own.

Perfect. The word was tossed around in pro football for decades. Look at that perfect play...perfect pass....We thought we knew what perfect was, but then the 1972 Dolphins came along and we realized the old standards just would not do.

The Dolphins were perfect in the literal sense of the word. Fourteen straight victories in the regular season, two wins in the AFC playoffs, followed by a 14-7 victory over Washington in Super Bowl VII. Seventeen-and-oh, the first unbeaten and untied team in NFL history.

It all started in the bitter aftermath of the Super Bowl loss to Dallas the previous January. Head coach Shula (who had moved to Miami in 1970) pressed that memory to his players' backsides like a branding iron. He built his landmark season on the sting of that defeat.

"I remember Shula talking to us after that [Dallas] game," said offensive tackle Norm Evans.

"He said, 'Everything you worked for all year, all the sprints you ran, all the iron you pumped, all the blood you shed, it's all for nothing now. There's only one thing to do and that's work that much harder next year, so we won't wind up in this position again.'

"Shula played on that. It was the first thing he brought up at our squad meeting the next training camp. He said, 'Remember how you felt after the Dallas game? OK, now is the time to do something about it. This is gonna be our year.'"

The 1972 Dolphins were not a flamboyant team. They were much like the Lombardi Packers: tough, smart, and disciplined. On offense, they stressed the running game with Larry Csonka and Jim Kiick. Butch and Sundance, as they fancied themselves. Eugene (Mercury) Morris provided the breakaway speed.

That year, the Dolphins rushed for 2,950 yards in 14 regular season games, an NFL record. What's more, Csonka and Morris each gained 1,000 yards, the first time two backs on the same team ever accomplished that feat.

On defense, the Dolphins adopted the identity of "No-Names." This stemmed from a remark Tom Landry made at Super Bowl VI: "I can't recall their names, but they are a matter of great concern to us."

Game VIII   **Miami Dolphins**

Game IX   **Pittsburgh Steelers**

Tackle Manny Fernandez, middle linebacker Nick Buoniconti, and safeties Jake Scott and Dick Anderson were not big names, but they were heady players in the Shula mold. They did not physically intimidate their opponents; rather, they killed them softly. They allowed just 181 points in the regular season and recorded three shutouts.

"This is the best football team I've ever faced," Washington head coach George Allen said. "Better than the 1966 Packers."

The strength of the Dolphins—not merely in talent, but also in character—was exemplified by the way they carried on after losing quarterback Bob Griese with a broken ankle in the fourth week of the season. Earl Morrall, who also had journeyed from Baltimore to Miami, took over and guided the Dolphins to 11 straight victories before giving way to Griese in the AFC title game.

Surprisingly, the Dolphins were three-point underdogs going into Super Bowl VII against Washington. The Redskins were just the opposite of the Dolphins, a colorful bunch of old-timers and good-timers, a team that had more miles on it than the Apollo 17 space capsule. But, like the Dolphins, the 'Skins knew how to win.

They had the league's leading rusher, Larry Brown, at tailback, and they had the NFL's all-time leading receiver, Charley Taylor, at split end. They had a gritty defense led by linebackers Jack Pardee and Chris Hanburger. And, of course, they had Allen, the psychologist and head coach, pulling the strings.

"We felt all along that 1972 was our year," Redskins safety Brig Owens said. "I remember beating Miami in a preseason game. As we were leaving the field, I told Jim Kiick, 'I'll see you in the Super Bowl.'

"Then we went to the Super Bowl and who do you think is the first person I saw when I went out to warm up? Jim Kiick. We looked at each other and laughed."

The Redskins came out for the game in their usual state of hyperventilation, jumping on each other during the introductions, pumping their fists in the air. The Dolphins, who approached games like Philharmonic musicians, looked on in amusement.

"We thought it was pretty comical," guard Larry Little said. "We saved our emotion for when the game started, when it counted."

Miami controlled the game from the beginning. Griese hit Howard Twilley for a touchdown late in the first quarter, then Kiick banged over from the 1 in the second quarter and, the way the Miami defense was playing, it looked like the 17-0 season was all but assured.

But, with two minutes to go, the game changed course. Miami's Garo Yepremian had a field goal attempt blocked by Bill Brundige. The little Cypriot scooped up the loose ball and, for reasons known only to him, he attempted the first, and last, forward pass of his NFL career.

The ball popped out of his hand, he slapped at it and watched helplessly as it fell into the arms of Washington's Mike Bass. Bass rumbled 49 yards to a touchdown and Curt Knight's conversion made it 14-7. There was laughter everywhere, except on the Miami bench.

"I went to the sidelines," Evans said, "and everybody, including Shula, was in a state of shock. I sat down, closed my eyes and, for the first time in my life, I actually prayed for a win. I said, 'Dear Lord, please don't make us do this year all over again.'"

"I don't know what happened," Yepremian said later. "My mind went blank."

The Redskins got the ball back with a minute to go and a chance to tie. Billy Kilmer completed a pass to Brown but he was sacked by defensive ends Vern Den Herder and

Game X   **Pittsburgh Steelers**

Bill Stanfill as time ran out.

Scott was voted most valuable player for two timely interceptions, but the award could have easily gone to Csonka who rushed for 112 yards, or Fernandez, who made a dozen unassisted tackles and shut down Brown.

If 17-0 was the ultimate, the next season was not far behind. The Dolphins lost two league games, but they were more impressive than ever in the playoffs, demolishing Cincinnati (34-16) and Oakland (27-10).

In Super Bowl VIII, they rolled over Minnesota 24-7 in Rice Stadium, Houston. The first two times they had the ball, the Dolphins drove the length of the field for touchdowns by Csonka, who finished with 145 yards rushing. Griese threw just seven passes, completing six.

"We ran the ball right down their throat," center Jim Langer said. "I'll never forget those first two drives. Thirteen minutes into the game and it was over. It was the best feeling I ever had as an offensive lineman.

"People often ask me if those Dolphins were the best [NFL] team ever. Who can say? But for those thirteen minutes, yeah, we might have been."

For 42 years, the Pittsburgh Steelers were the NFL's child of scorn. They never won so much as a division championship. They came close a few times—once under Jock Sutherland in the 1940s, once under Buddy Parker in the 1960s—but they never quite made it.

In 1969, Dan Rooney, son of beloved team founder Art Rooney, was named president of the Steelers. One of his first moves was to hire a Baltimore assistant, Chuck Noll, as his head coach. Rooney stuck with Noll through a tortuous 1-13 season. Rooney watched as his new head coach—a low-key, all-business type—rebuilt the Steelers through the draft.

The Steelers made the AFC playoffs in 1972 and stunned Oakland in the divisional playoffs on Franco Harris's famous Immaculate Reception. They lost the AFC title game to Miami's team of destiny, but they left an impression. "That Pittsburgh team," Shula said, "is going to be something."

In 1974, the Steelers won their first conference championship, knocking off Oakland in the final playoff game. On January 12, 1975, they went to Super Bowl IX against Minnesota. It was a time of deliverance for the older Steelers, the ones who had endured the years of putdowns and frustrations.

"You wait that long for something," center Ray Mansfield said, "you sure as hell aren't gonna let it get away."

"I'll never forget walking out of that locker room," defensive tackle Mean Joe Greene said, recalling that blustery day at Tulane Stadium. "The Vikings were standing in the tunnel, waiting to be introduced. There we were, all eighty of us, jammed together in this narrow walkway.

"We [the Steelers] were loose and joking around. The Vikings were standing there stone-faced. They looked like they were at attention. I saw Alan Page. I smiled and said hello. He didn't say anything.

"I remember Glen Edwards, our free safety, was trying to talk to the [Minnesota] guy next to him. The guy wouldn't answer. He just kept staring straight ahead. Finally, Glen said, 'OK, big fella. You'd better buckle up 'cause you're in for a long day.'

"That was the way we all felt. We felt there was no way the Vikings were gonna beat us. We had a game plan that [linebacker] Andy Russell said could've fallen off the shelf and killed a dog. It was that strong.

"The only thing we weren't prepared for was the weather," Greene added. "It was

Game XI   **Oakland Raiders**

Game XII   **Dallas Cowboys**

nice and warm all week, but it turned cold the day of the game. We didn't have our heavy uniforms with us. I went out in a summer jersey with the short sleeves.

"The wind hit me and it made goose bumps come up on my arm. I was standing in the tunnel and there was this Minnesota fan right there in the first row. He looked at my arms and he started hollering, 'Look. Mean Joe's scared. Look at the goose bumps on his arm.'

"That made me so damn mad. I wasn't afraid. Hell, I couldn't wait to get out there. But here was this guy telling everybody in that end of the stadium that Mean Joe Greene was getting goose bumps. It was embarrassing.''

That was nothing compared with the embarrassment Minnesota suffered once the game began. The Vikings managed just 17 yards rushing against the Steel Curtain defense. They were outgained by the Steelers 333 net yards to 119. The final score—Pittsburgh 16, Minnesota 6—doesn't begin to reflect the Steelers' domination.

The next year, the Steelers returned to the Super Bowl and met up with the Cowboys, the first wild card team to reach the finals. The game commenced with Dallas running a reverse—to rookie linebacker Thomas (Hollywood) Henderson, no less—on the opening kickoff.

That set the pattern for the frenetic afternoon. Two proud football teams let it all hang out for 60 minutes and the result was the best Super Bowl to date, a swift, savage game that left the sellout crowd and the national television audience limp.

It was a game that will be remembered for the acrobatics of Lynn Swann, who made four catches for 161 yards. It will be remembered for the courage of Roger Staubach, who played brilliantly despite injured ribs. And it will be remembered for the raging presence of Jack Lambert, who refused to let the Steelers die.

The Cowboys were leading 10-7 in the second quarter and the Steelers were sagging. Greene was out with a pinched nerve and the club missed his leadership, his "let's-get-down-and-kick-ass" cockiness. Lambert, the middle linebacker, took over.

"I felt we were intimidated a little bit in the first half," Lambert said. "The Pittsburgh Steelers aren't supposed to be intimidated. We're supposed to be the intimidators. I decided to do something about it.''

When Roy Gerela missed a field goal, Dallas safety Cliff Harris patted him on the helmet, offering mock congratulations. Lambert reacted immediately, grabbing Harris by the neck and hurling him to the ground. Lambert's meting out of street corner justice ignited the Steelers.

The Pittsburgh defense swarmed all over the Cowboys. Reggie Harrison blocked Mitch Hoopes's punt for a safety. Moments later, a heavy rush forced Staubach to throw into the coverage. Safety Mike Wagner intercepted and returned deep into Dallas territory. Two field goals by Gerela and the Steelers were ahead 15-10.

Lambert was in the middle of everything: setting his front four, hurling himself into the line, garroting receivers over the middle, taunting any Dallas player who crossed his path.

"Lambert was phenomenal," Staubach said. "He was in and out of the line. Our blockers couldn't get to him. And he was very vocal.''

Late in the game, Bradshaw decided to put it away. On third-and-four, he called a deep post to Swann. The Cowboys were in full blitz with linebacker D.D. Lewis and Harris coming. Lewis was picked up, but Harris roared through untouched. He cracked Bradshaw in the jaw just as he released the ball.

Swann was covered one-on-one by cornerback Mark Washington. Washington had good position but Swann climbed that invisible staircase once again to pull the ball

down. The play went for a 64-yard touchdown but Bradshaw never saw it. He was knocked out cold. He didn't know the score until 10 minutes later when he awoke in the locker room.

By then, the Cowboys had cut the lead to four (21-17) and they were driving again. The game ended with Staubach throwing into the end zone for Drew Pearson, and Edwards intercepting and running out the clock with his return. Across the nation, 100 million hearts went off hold.

It was a classic game, the kind that begged for a rematch. The sequel was three years in the making, but well worth the wait. Pittsburgh and Dallas, the Ali and Frazier of pro football, met again at the Orange Bowl, this time in Super Bowl XIII.

Dallas was on a roll. It had beaten Denver in convincing fashion, 27-10, the year before in Super Bowl XII. The Cowboys' offense came up with the big plays while their Doomsday II defense, led by co-most valuable players Harvey Martin and Randy White, dominated the Broncos, intercepting Craig Morton four times and recovering four fumbles. But once the Cowboys took the field against the Steelers that January 21 of 1979, that game was forgotten; the drama picked up right where it had left off in 1976.

Bradshaw passed 28 yards to John Stallworth for one touchdown. Staubach passed to Tony Hill to tie. Linebacker Mike Hegman stole the ball from Bradshaw's arms and ran 37 yards for a touchdown. Bradshaw hit Stallworth, who broke a tackle and raced 75 yards to score again. And this was all in the first 20 minutes.

"It was a game where we could never seem to catch our breath," Pittsburgh safety Wagner said. "It was back and forth, back and forth, like a basketball game. It was one of those days where you knew no lead was gonna be safe."

Rocky Bleier made a leaping, fingertip catch of a Bradshaw pass to put the Steelers up 21-14 at the half. The Cowboys came back in the third quarter and drove toward the Pittsburgh goal line. Then came the play everyone remembers; the play that foreshadowed the Cowboys' fate.

Staubach faked a handoff, rolled out, and found tight end Jackie Smith alone in the end zone. Smith was a former St. Louis Cardinal, a pro's pro who waited 14 years for his one shot at a Super Bowl ring. How nice, everyone said, that Jackie could go out a winner. That's what they were saying just before Staubach threw that pass.

The ball hit Smith in the chest and fell to the ground. Staubach, who seldom reacts to such things, grabbed his helmet. Tom Landry threw back his head and stared into the sky. Smith seemed to freeze in mid-air, his arms locked at his sides, his face contorted in anguish. The Drop Heard 'Round the World, it was called.

The Cowboys settled for a field goal, but it left them four points down going into the final period. When Franco scored on a 22-yard run and Swann pulled down an 18-yard touchdown pass from Bradshaw, the Steelers stretched their lead to 35-17 and, back in Pittsburgh, the victory party began.

The boys from the mills were so busy hoisting their cans of Iron City, they hardly noticed the Cowboys get one touchdown back on Staubach's pass to Billy Joe DuPree. And they didn't pay much attention when the Cowboys recovered the onside kick. Aw, it's the last couple minutes. Who cares? Garbage time, right?

But then the Cowboys scored again—Staubach to Butch Johnson—and, suddenly, the Steelers' lead was down to four (35-31). There were 26 seconds left, the Cowboys were lining up for another onside kick, and the taprooms and parlors of Pittsburgh fell silent. Staubach had that eerie glow around him, like all he needed was one or two more plays and he could pull it out.

Game XIV   **Pittsburgh Steelers**

Game XV   **Oakland Raiders**

Rafael Septien squibbed his kickoff, but Bleier recovered. The Steelers ran out the clock and thus became the first team to win three Super Bowls. Bradshaw, who threw for 318 yards and four touchdowns, was named most valuable player.

Those two Steelers-Cowboys thrillers set the standard against which all future Super Bowls would be measured. No one expected Super Bowl XIV, Pittsburgh versus Los Angeles, to come close. In fact, it conjured up images of the first two Super Bowls, back when competitive balance ended with the pregame coin toss.

The Rams had the poorest record ever for a Super Bowl participant: nine wins, seven losses. They beat Dallas on big (some considered them lucky) plays in the playoffs 21-19, then struggled through Tampa Bay 9-0 to the NFC championship. The oddsmakers made the Rams 11-point underdogs, even though the game would be played on local turf in Pasadena's Rose Bowl.

The Los Angeles quarterback was Vince Ferragamo, a handsome, young chap starting only his sixth pro game. The Pittsburgh defense viewed Vince the way a kindergarten class might view a Twinkie. The Steel Curtain figured to swarm Ferragamo, smack him around, and then devour him, dimples and all.

But the Rams had a different scenario in mind. They took the lead in the first quarter on a one-yard plunge by Cullen Bryant, then they went ahead 13-10 at halftime on two field goals by Frank Corral. Halfback Wendell Tyler broke away on a 39-yard run and, gradually, it began to dawn on the Steelers, "Hey, we're in a football game."

"The Rams were a fired-up team," the Steelers' Greene recalled. "And it wasn't one of those locker room highs that lasts three minutes. Those guys were pumped.

"That was the first time I could ever remember playing against a team that was more intense than we were. They came out and ran the ball on us. They were beating us in the trenches, moving us out. We were shocked. At halftime, we were back on our heels.

"Terry got up in the locker room and, for the first time in his career, he spoke up. He said, 'Look, we know we've got the better team. We've just gotta play with more intensity. We've gotta take it to them, and play Steeler football.' It worked. The guys responded."

However, the Rams, spurred on by a partisan crowd of 103,985, hung tough. Early in the third quarter, Bradshaw hit Swann for a 47-yard touchdown to put Pittsburgh ahead. Then Lawrence McCutcheon threw a halfback option pass to Ron Smith to put the Rams ahead. The lead changed hands six times in all.

In the fourth quarter, the Steelers were trailing and Swann, their big-play man, was out with a concussion. Bradshaw looked to the other side where Stallworth was running a post pattern, one step behind cornerback Rod Perry and safety Dave Elmendorf. Bradshaw laid the ball in Stallworth's arms and he pulled away to complete a spectacular 73-yard scoring play.

"We tried that play in practice a dozen times this week and never completed it," Bradshaw said. "I didn't have much confidence in it, but Chuck [Noll] called it and there it was."

The Rams could have crumbled after that bomb, but they didn't. Ferragamo drove his team to the Steelers' 32 and was threatening to regain the lead when he forced a pass into the middle. Lambert stepped in front of Smith and intercepted at the 14.

Bradshaw completed another long pass to Stallworth, got an interference call at the goal line, and, three plays later, Harris rolled in for the clinching touchdown. The Steelers won 31-19, but it was a struggle. Bradshaw, again the most valuable player,

was so burned out, he talked about retiring after the game.

"We won that game for one reason—we had more good players," Greene said. "We wore the Rams down, but it was a war. It was much tougher than the two Dallas games. Physically, emotionally, every way there is.

"We had a victory party back at our hotel, but we were too drained to do much of anything. Terry, L.C. [Greenwood], Lambert, and myself, we were all out of it. I couldn't tell if we had won or just survived."

The game has changed in the last few years. The new scheduling format and the quest for parity make it more difficult than ever to establish a dynasty in the NFL. We may never again see a team win four Super Bowls in six years the way the Steelers did in the 1970s.

The trend now is for the annual team of destiny to swoop down from the balcony, grab the Lombardi Trophy, and vanish, just that quickly, into the shadows. There are no long reigns, nor long goodbyes. Just some interesting surprises.

The Raiders were not exactly unknown in January, 1981, when they went to Super Bowl XV against Philadelphia. They were making their third appearance in the big game and had already won one NFL title, defeating Minnesota with ease 32-14 in Super Bowl XI. In that game, the overwhelming Raiders had scored touchdowns on both offense and defense, gained a Super Bowl record 429 total yards, and held the Vikings to just 71 yards on the ground. But they came through the back door to meet the Eagles.

The Pride and Poise gang from Oakland had fallen on hard times. They missed the playoffs the previous two years and they had to travel the wild card route to Super Sunday in New Orleans. They were led by a quarterback, Jim Plunkett, who was waived by two other teams and was mildewing on their bench until Dan Pastorini broke his leg four weeks into the season.

This wasn't the slick, fearsome machine we normally associate with the Raiders, but it was plenty good enough to defeat the Eagles, 27-10, for the championship. Plunkett was the most valuable player and if the sight of him leaving the field in the embrace of head coach Tom Flores didn't touch your heart, then your insides must be under warranty with Frigidare.

Plunkett had come back from surgery and the unemployment line to win his Super Bowl. The man refused to quit when quitting would have been the easy, even logical, thing to do. He taught us all an eloquent lesson in the human spirit, a lesson that often courage and stubbornness are one and the same.

"My story is no different than anyone else's," Plunkett said. "I was in the right place at the right time. I'm not a real emotional person, I don't jump up and down, but I'm as happy as I can be right now."

The next year, the Raiders fell to 7-9 and Plunkett lost his starting job to rookie Marc Wilson. The torch was gathered up by the team from the other side of the Bay, the San Francisco 49ers. The 49ers, winners of just 10 games the previous three years, went to Super Bowl XVI to face the Cincinnati Bengals.

It was an unlikely matchup—both teams were 6-10 in 1980—in an unlikely setting, the Silverdome in Pontiac, Michigan. It marked the first time the Super Bowl was played in a northern city. It was the first time the game's Roman numeral was higher than the local temperature at kickoff; the first time the stadium, not the Scotch, was on the rocks.

On Super Sunday, the wind chill factor was below zero and the Silverdome parking

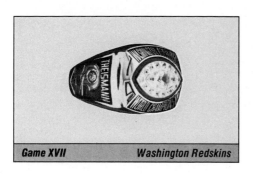

Game XVII   **Washington Redskins**

lot looked like the luge course at Lake Placid, but inside the 49ers were smoking. They opened a 20-0 halftime lead on the Bengals, then held on to win 26-21.

Joe Montana became the tenth quarterback, the fifth in a row, to win the car as most valuable player. The former Notre Dame star had a fine day, passing for one touchdown, running for another, but when San Francisco fans remember the game, they think of two things: The Catch by Dwight Clark that beat Dallas in the playoffs to put the 49ers in the Super Bowl, and The Goal-Line Stand that ultimately may have won it for them.

The 49ers' defense, chock full of rookies and mistrusted much of the season, put the kabosh on Cincinnati's comeback plans in the third quarter. The Bengals had first-and-goal at the 3, then second-and-goal at the 7. On third down quarterback Ken Anderson swung a pass out to running back Charles Alexander, who was met with irresistible force just shy of the goal line, and stopped cold, by linebacker Dan Bunz. On fourth down, the entire 49ers defense seemed to converge at the ball carrier. No touchdown.

Pete Johnson, the 260-pound fullback who looks like he should be mounted on treads, was stacked up three of the four plays by the tenacious 49ers.

"That play worked for us all year," Johnson said of his fourth-down try. "There was no reason to assume it wouldn't work today. You've gotta give the 49ers credit. They played it tough."

The 1982 season followed, hollow and bitter. The players' strike cut seven weeks off the schedule and everyone lost, particularly the 49ers. They finished 3-6 and became the third straight defending Super Bowl champion team to miss the playoffs.

The Washington Redskins, another surprise team, represented the NFC in Super Bowl XVII. The Miami Dolphins, with Shula making his fifth Super Bowl appearance, represented the AFC.

The pregame hype read like a Marvel comic book, what with all the talk about the Hogs (the Washington offensive linemen) tussling with the Killer Bees defense (Bob Baumhower, Doug Betters, the Blackwood brothers, et al). Then there were the Washington Smurfs (the smallish receivers) and the Fun Bunch. Who was coaching the Redskins anyway, Jim Henson?

Washington won the game 27-17, as fullback John Riggins carried 38 times for 166 yards, both Super Bowl records. Riggins put the game away in the fourth quarter, breaking a fourth-and-one carry around left end, shaking off cornerback Don McNeal like a cellophane wrapper and pounding 43 yards to the end zone.

"John Riggins was Mr. Universe, Mr. All-World," said Betters, the Miami defensive end. "He was the MVP today. Their offense was no secret: Give it to John. They have a good line, but it's Riggins that makes 'em go."

Yeah, they play for the trophies. They play for the diamond rings and, of course, the big bucks. But Super Bowl is more than that. After four trips to the mountaintop, Joe Greene knows the terrain, and the emotion, better than anyone.

"There is nothing in life to compare to the Super Bowl," Greene said. "That's the carrot that hangs in front of you every season. That's what carries you through twenty games, then the playoffs.

"The Super Bowl is a happening. The excitement, the intensity. All week, the air is thick with it. Then there's the game. The atmosphere in the stadium right before kickoff is unbelievable. It takes your breath away.

"The thrill never wears off," Greene said. "If you go once, it makes you want it that much more the next year. I still get mad when I think about the ones I missed. It's like somebody came along those years and stole my Christmas."

Games

Super Bowl photographs are meant to be savored. They tell their stories over and over, yet, like your father's old jokes, you never tire of them. Jim O'Brien's exultant victory leap after kicking the field goal that won Game V. The triangle of power formed as Manny Fernandez, neck cords straining, halts bulldozing Larry Brown. The intense concentration of a diving Butch Johnson, reflected thousands of times over in the blur of the background crowd, as the ball settles remarkably into his outstretched hands. These are the moments that justify the ''super'' in Super Bowl.

The photographs, though, are but fragments, shiny coins that jingle. It is the games themselves that are the hard currency of memory, each with its own denomination, each with its own perceived value.

Which game is worth the most? Well, Game I because it was the first, the showdown between the old league and the new. And Game III because it was the upset game, youth refusing to believe the odds. And Game VII because it was the ''perfect'' game, when the dream of an unbeaten record came true. And Game XIII because it was such a classic, the confrontation that had it all. And Game XVII because. . . . Hold on. Choosing the best Super Bowl, like picking the best of anything, is not necessarily the most gainful pursuit. Each game has something to recommend it, something that sets it apart and gives it a distinct tangibility. Better would be to think of the 17 Super Bowl games—and the photographs that document them—as a stunning portfolio, a catalog of works that grows richer every year.

Green Bay won Super Bowl I, much to the relief of anxious NFL owners, but the victory didn't come without a few surprises. Though fullback Jim Taylor (31, previous page) ran the Packers' trademark sweep with his usual ferocity, the defense had to resort to uncharacteristic blitzes to disrupt the Chiefs' offense. And though Bart Starr passed with his usual precision, he didn't throw to his regular receivers; veteran Max McGee (85, left) came off the bench in the first quarter to replace injured wide receiver Boyd Dowler, and caught seven passes, two for touchdowns. In the Packers' jubilant locker room after the game, NFL Commissioner Pete Rozelle presented beaming Vince Lombardi the AFL-NFL World Championship Trophy (above) that would later be named in the coach's honor.

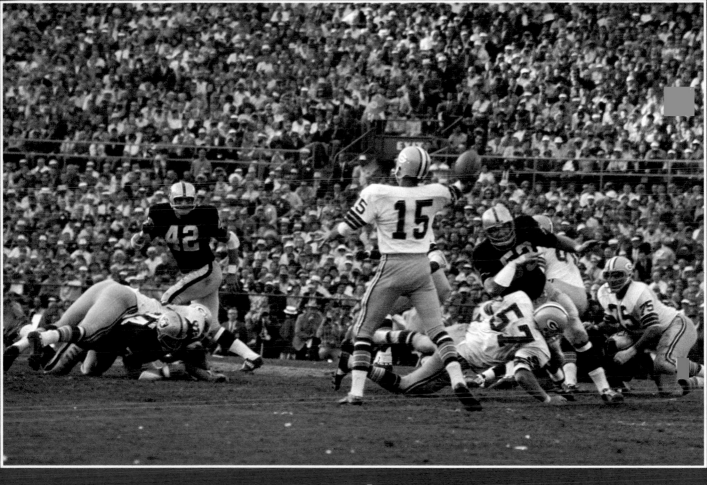

In a tale of two quarterbacks, the teams around them made all the difference. Opposing Super Bowl II quarterbacks Daryle Lamonica (3) of Oakland (left) and Bart Starr (15) of Green Bay (above) finished the game with almost identical passing statistics. However, in Vince Lombardi's final game as Green Bay's head coach, the veteran Packers played inspired football, while the young Raiders were forced to play catch-up.

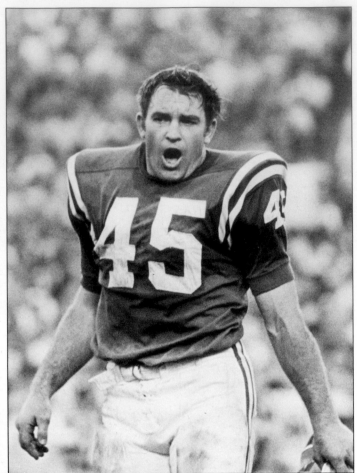

There isn't much that can be said about Game III for the Baltimore Colts; where words fail, photographs of anger, frustration, disbelief, and discouragement are eloquent. The Colts went into the game as NFL champions, powerful and confident. Perhaps they were too confident, or their opponents, the New York Jets, were too young and proud to fear them. But almost from the start, Baltimore's world championship dream turned into the self-imposed ignominy of being the first NFL team to lose a Super Bowl.

*T*he Jets' offense kept the Colts reeling with the brilliant play calling of quarterback Joe Namath (12, left)—most frequently in the form of audibles at the line of scrimmage—and the power running of Matt Snell (41, above) behind an aroused line. The mistakes (four interceptions and a costly fumble) that plagued the Baltimore offense were compounded by the exasperation of a team of winners who refused to believe they could lose.

The Kansas City offense was armed and dangerous at Super Bowl IV. Running back Mike Garrett (21) scored one touchdown on a five-yard run (left), ran consistently, and caught two passes. Wide receiver Otis Taylor caught six passes, one for a 46-yard touchdown. Frank Pitts, the other wide receiver, caught three passes, and, more important, gained 37 yards on three devastating reverses. And kicker Jan Stenerud came through on three first-half field goals, including a 48-yarder for the first score of the game. But it wasn't the pistol-hot Chiefs offense that made the Vikings misfire. It was the big guns of the Chiefs' defensive line—ends Aaron Brown and Jerry Mays, and tackles Buck Buchanan and Curley Culp—who were most instrumental in the victory.

Quarterback Len Dawson (16) was the focus of attention for more than his Kansas City teammates in the huddle. Playing Game IV under allegations, later dismissed, of involvement with a nationwide ring of gamblers, Dawson spent much of Super Bowl week in seclusion. In the face of emotional trauma, Dawson (a.k.a. ''Lenny the Cool'') kept his poise, completing 70 percent of his passes. He earned the game's most valuable player award, and helped even the record at two Super Bowls apiece for the AFL and NFL in the final game before the leagues merged.

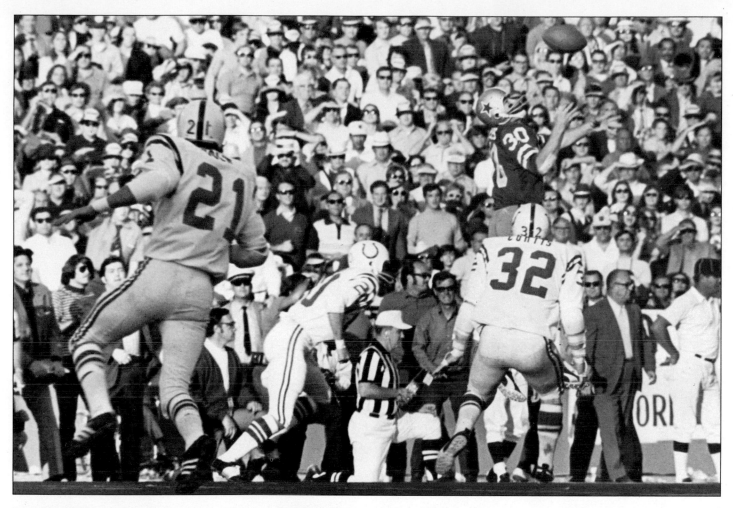

*A*gony turned to ecstasy in two years for the Baltimore Colts as they returned to the Super Bowl for Game V to face the Dallas Cowboys. It was ironic, considering their earlier loss to the Jets, that the Colts were representing the AFC under the new post-merger alignment. In a game of errors, the final error cost the Cowboys a victory. A muffed pass, intercepted by Colts middle linebacker Mike Curtis (32, above), led to a game-winning field goal with five seconds left. Kicker Jim O'Brien (80, opposite) and holder Earl Morrall expressed the jubilation of the Colts, while Mel Renfro (left) and the Cowboys were left to brood for another year.

Though two of Dallas's three touchdowns in Super Bowl VI came on passes, the game was fought—and ultimately won— on the ground. On offense, the Cowboys simply ran over the Dolphins; they rushed for 252 yards, mostly on the combined efforts of running backs Duane Thomas, Calvin Hill, and Walt Garrison (32, left) and scrambling quarterback Roger Staubach (12, opposite), who was named the game's MVP. On defense, Bob Lilly and his linemates closed off the middle, allowing Miami just 80 rushing yards. Head coach Tom Landry (below) flashed a rare smile, prompted probably as much by relief at the loss of the Cowboys' "chokers" image as by his postgame victory ride.

NFL theory has it that defense not only gets teams to the big games, but wins them as well. Super Bowl VII, the culmination of Miami's perfect 17-0 season, stands as a well-constructed proof of that theory. Dolphins safety Jake Scott (13, above) picked off two of Washington quarterback Billy Kilmer's passes on critical drives. Up on the line, Manny Fernandez (75, right) personally kept NFL rushing leader Larry Brown under wraps. "Manny played the finest game I've ever seen a tackle play," said Miami head coach Don Shula. "It was as if he took the line of scrimmage and pushed it one yard back into their backfield."

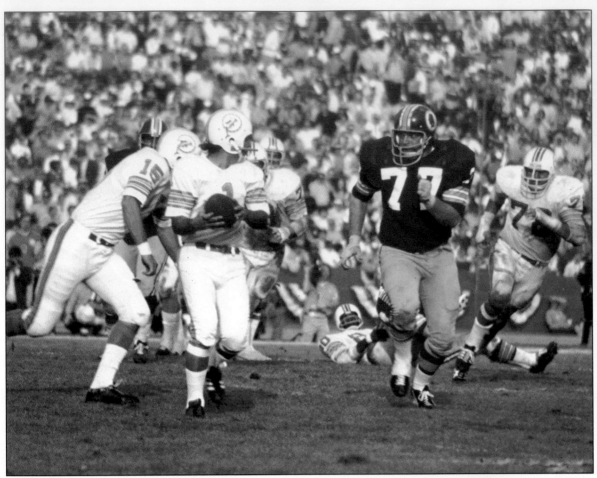

*S*cott and Fernandez may have been the heroes of Game VII, but Miami kicker Garo Yepremian, the man who was nearly the goat, may be better remembered. When Yepremian (1) attempted a late fourth-quarter field goal, the kick was blocked by Bill Brundige. Yepremian then scooped up the ball, rolled out (above), and flubbed a pass (right). The Redskins' Mike Bass (41, opposite) recovered the ball and took it 49 yards to avert a shutout.

VIII

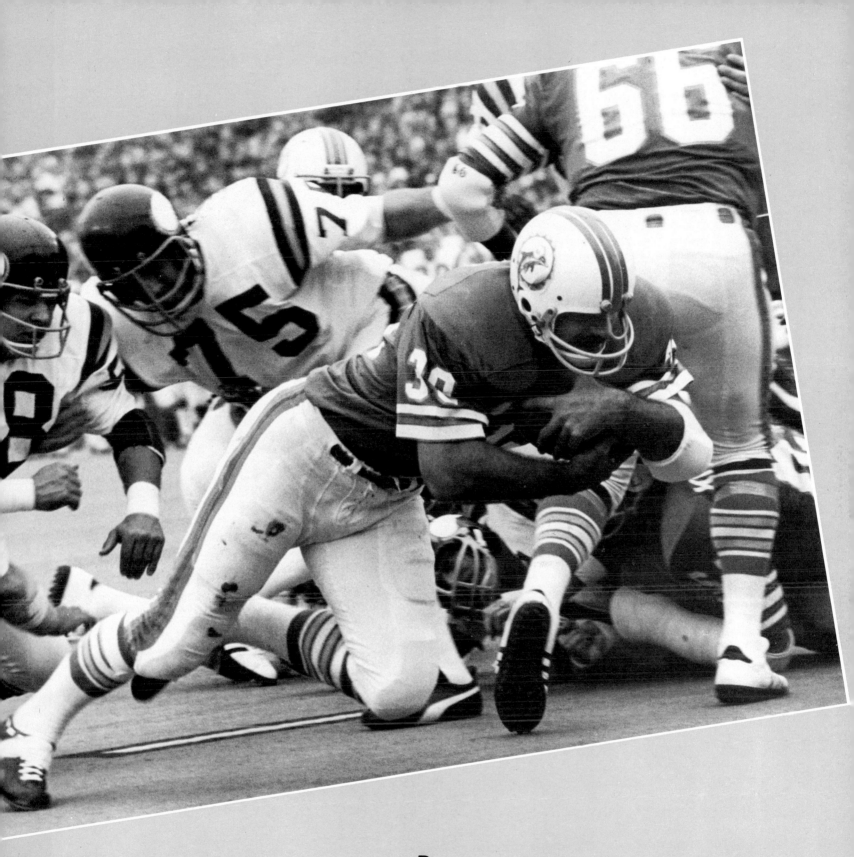

*D*espite Minnesota defensive tackle Alan Page's (88, left) protest of a penalty call, there could be little argument over the outcome of Game VIII. The Vikings got whipped, pure and simple, as the Dolphins became the first team since the Packers to win back-to-back Super Bowls. Much of the damage was done by bruising Miami fullback Larry Csonka (above), who ran for a record 145 yards and two touchdowns behind an offensive line that gave Minnesota's Purple People Eaters indigestion.

Game IX was Minnesota's third Super Bowl in six years. Pittsburgh had waited 42 years just to get a shot at an NFL championship. It appeared early that the Steelers might have to wait some more; at the end of the first half they led the powerful and more experienced Vikings by only a small 2-0 margin after Dwight White tackled quarterback Fran Tarkenton (10, right) in the end zone for a safety. But Pittsburgh drew its Steel Curtain defense tightly closed in the second half, limiting the Vikings to a meager total of 17 yards rushing and 102 yards passing all day.

IX

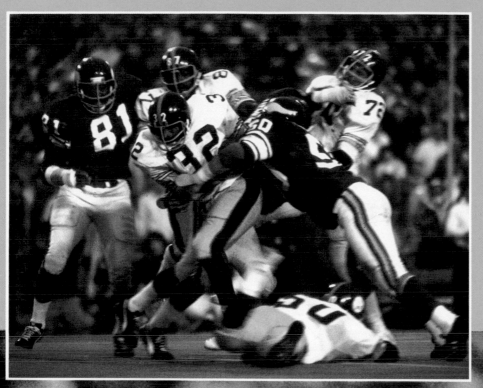

There was plenty of steel in the Steelers' offense, too. Running back Franco Harris (32, left) broke Larry Csonka's one-year-old rushing record with 158 yards on 34 carries, and scored one touchdown. Harris's backfield mate, gutty Rocky Bleier, contributed 65 yards rushing and caught two passes. Right guard Gerry Mullins was out in front of Harris and Bleier much of the way. And through it all, Terry Bradshaw (12, below), tempered by a season-long battle to regain his starter status, established himself as Pittsburgh's once and future quarterback.

The makings of a dynasty were confirmed in Game X when the Steelers returned to the Super Bowl and defeated the Cowboys in an all-out war. The tone of the afternoon was typified by the fourth-quarter touchdown play that put the game away for Pittsburgh. As Terry Bradshaw let fly a long bomb, he was hit and knocked unconscious by blitzing Dallas safety Cliff Harris. The pass soared true; wide receiver Lynn Swann outjumped safety Mark Washington for the ball and a 64-yard score. While Swann, his teammates, and Steelers fans celebrated (inset), Bradshaw, oblivious to the outcome of the play, had to be helped from the field (left).

Swann (88, above) made remarkable catches seem almost routine at Super Bowl X. He was named the game's most valuable player for his four acrobatic receptions for 161 yards. Aerial feats aside, the victory belonged in large measure once again to the Pittsburgh defense. Inspired by middle linebacker Jack Lambert, who played like a man possessed, the Steelers' defensive linemen went after quarterback Roger Staubach, sacking him seven times and intercepting three of his passes. Dallas rushers and receivers didn't fare much better at the hands of outside linebackers Andy Russell (34, right) and Jack Ham (59).

Oakland Raiders tight end Dave Casper (87, opposite) reaches for a touchdown pass at Super Bowl XI; his head coach, John Madden (above) reaches for the clouds in a gesture of victory after the game. But for the Minnesota Vikings, who came up short in their fourth Super Bowl bid, there were no silver linings, only soft words of consolation from guard Charles Goodrum (68, left) to running back Chuck Foreman (44), on the verge of tears.

Big plays were de rigueur for the Cowboys on offense and defense in Super Bowl XII. One of the biggest was wide receiver Butch Johnson's diving fingertip touchdown catch (left) in the third quarter. The game was initially billed as a defensive battle, Denver's Orange Crush versus Dallas's Doomsday II. Unfortunately for the Cinderella Broncos and quarterback Craig Morton (7), doomsday came early and often, in the form of Ed (Too Tall) Jones (72, above), Jethro Pugh, and the game's co-most valuable players, Harvey Martin and Randy White.

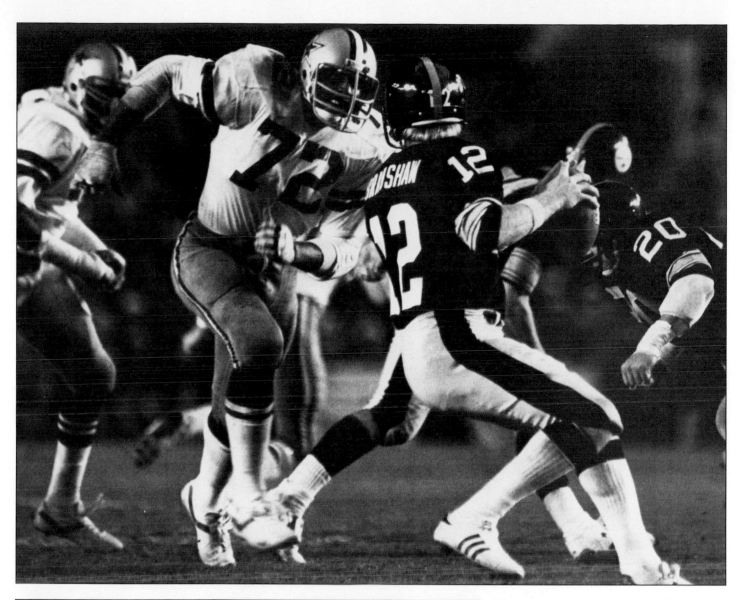

Super Bowl XIII was a lucky one for fans. Not only was it the first Super Bowl rematch, it was that rarity (rare at least in movies) where the sequel emerged better than the original. Pittsburgh and Dallas picked up on the action from Game X, and produced what is considered the most exciting Super Bowl of all. Terry Bradshaw (12) took a few knocks from the Dallas pass rush, but thanks to consistently fine protection from his front line, was able to connect on passes for 318 yards and four touchdowns. Running back Rocky Bleier and wide receiver Lynn Swann each caught one touchdown pass; wide receiver John Stallworth (82, left) caught two, one a 10-yard reception he turned into a 75-yard score.

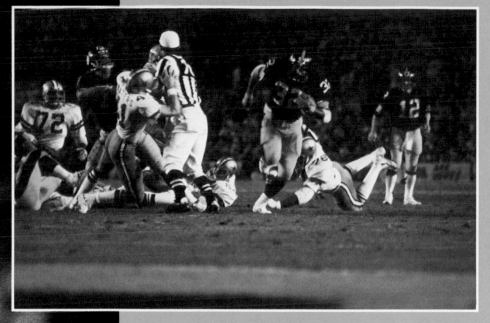

In one of Game XIII's most crucial plays— perhaps the turning point for the Cowboys —veteran tight end Jackie Smith's luck ran out. Wide open in the end zone, Smith (81, far left) couldn't hold on to Roger Staubach's short pass and became the picture of frozen anguish. Pittsburgh running back Franco Harris reacted strongly himself to the Cowboys' rough handling of Terry Bradshaw. Harris took out his anger by going 22 yards through the heart of a Dallas blitz (sequence) for a telling fourth-quarter touchdown.

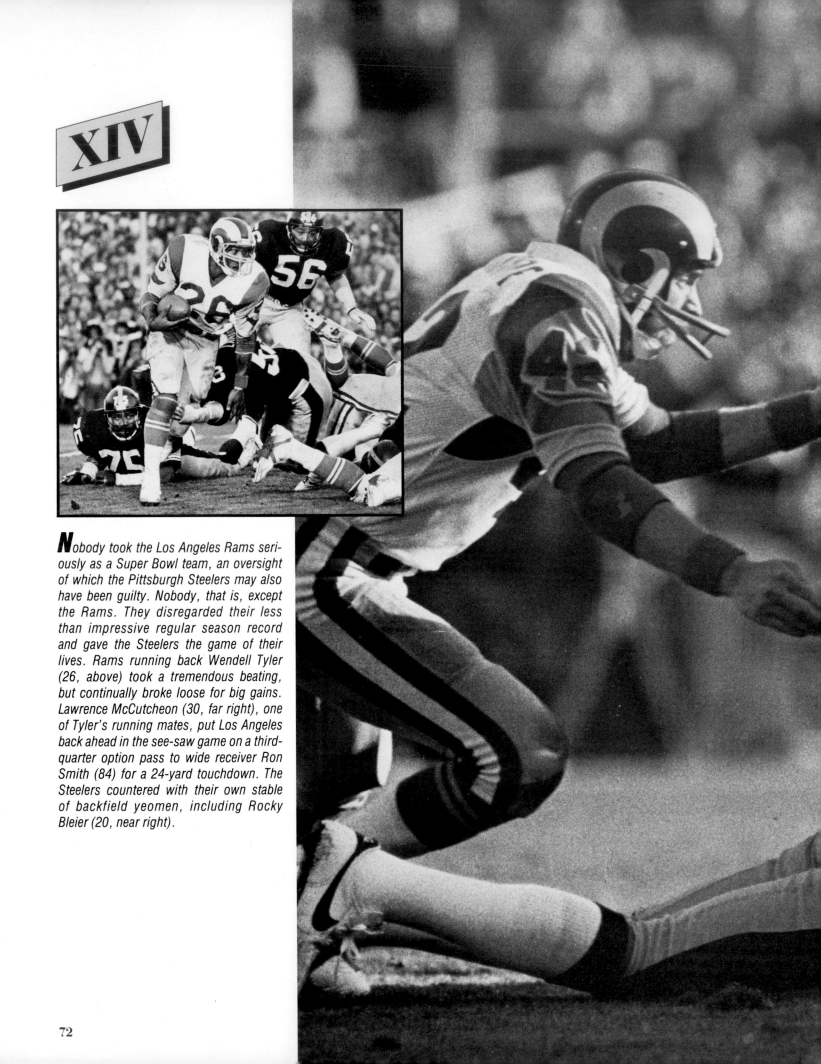

XIV

Nobody took the Los Angeles Rams seriously as a Super Bowl team, an oversight of which the Pittsburgh Steelers may also have been guilty. Nobody, that is, except the Rams. They disregarded their less than impressive regular season record and gave the Steelers the game of their lives. Rams running back Wendell Tyler (26, above) took a tremendous beating, but continually broke loose for big gains. Lawrence McCutcheon (30, far right), one of Tyler's running mates, put Los Angeles back ahead in the see-saw game on a third-quarter option pass to wide receiver Ron Smith (84) for a 24-yard touchdown. The Steelers countered with their own stable of backfield yeomen, including Rocky Bleier (20, near right).

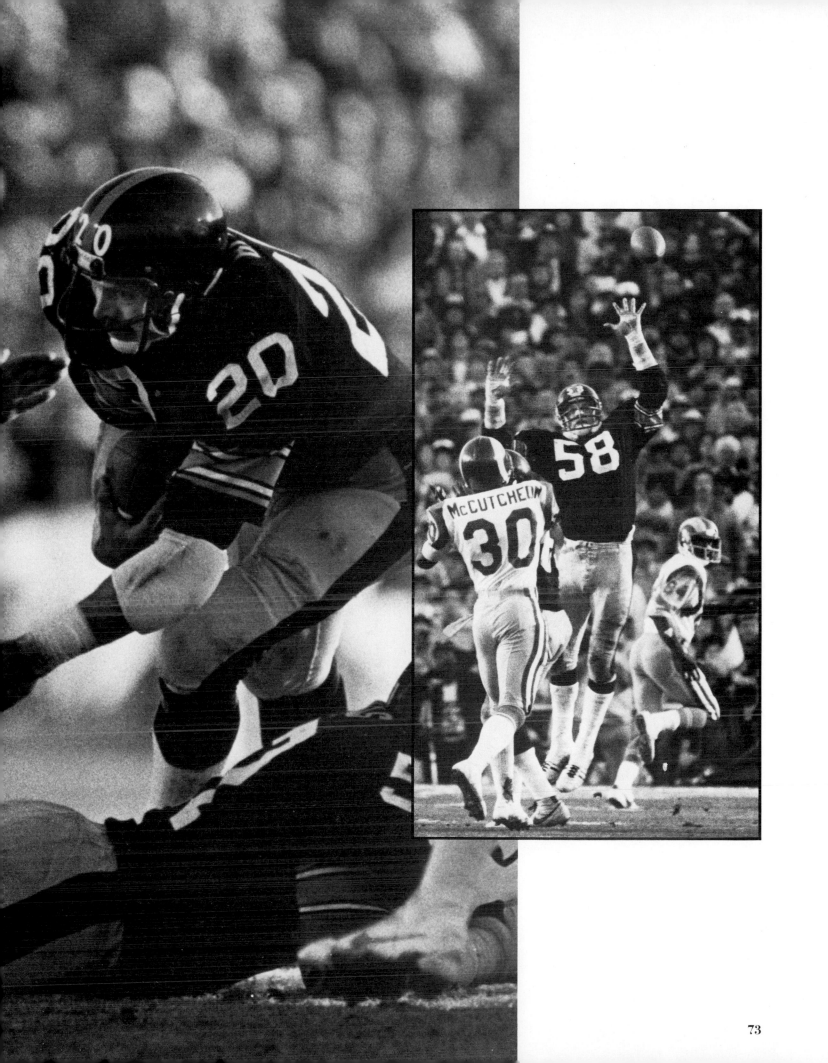

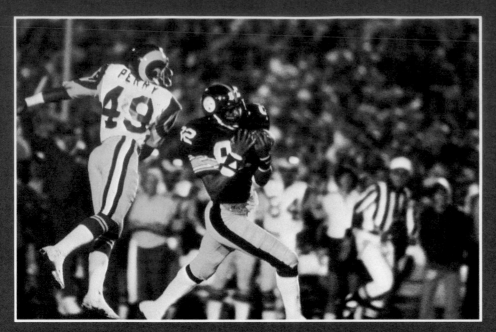

Other keys to Pittsburgh's eventual hard-fought victory in Super Bowl XIV, its fourth in six years, were the kick returns of Larry Anderson (five for a record 162 yards), Jack Lambert's late interception that stopped a critical Rams' drive, and the exceptional play of wide receiver John Stallworth. Though Stallworth only caught three passes, they went for 121 yards, one touchdown, and set up another score. The touchdown play (sequence) covered 73 yards as Stallworth (82) outstepped cornerback Rod Perry and left him sprawling on the way to the end zone.

XV

*O*nly the Raiders could have pulled it off—to have gone to the Super Bowl as a wild card team and won. Super Bowl XV belonged to them all the way; the Eagles and quarterback Ron Jaworski (7, far left), pressured from all sides by the Raiders' defense, never got off the ground. From the third play of the game, when Oakland linebacker Rod Martin made the first of his three interceptions, to linebacker Ted Hendricks's block of Tony Franklin's field goal attempt to end the first half (below), to wide receiver Cliff Branch's (21, center) third-quarter leaping catch in the end zone, to the final gun, the Raiders were in total control.

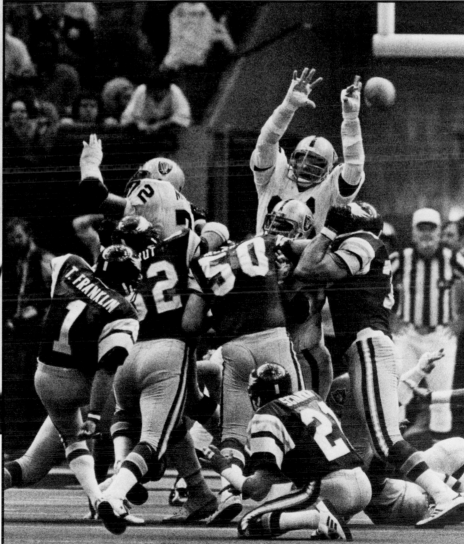

Super Bowl XVI featured two teams that, judging from their identical 6-10 records the previous year, were long-shot picks as contenders. But there they were at the Pontiac Silverdome, San Francisco and Cincinnati. At least they both were there for the second half. The first half was all 49ers, humming offensively, with quarterback Joe Montana (16, right), and defensively to the tune of a 20-0 halftime lead. Bengals quarterback Ken Anderson countered by running for a touchdown and passing for two more to tight end Dan Ross (89, above). But San Francisco stopped Cincinnati when it counted with a dramatic goal line stand (opposite).

XVII

*T*he domino theory met the Super Bowl record book at Game XVII, when Washington met Miami at the Rose Bowl. Each team did its share of game breaking and record breaking—24 new marks were set in all. Wide receiver Jimmy Cefalo (81, right) caught a pass from Dolphins quarterback David Woodley at the Miami 45 and took it in for an early score. Fulton Walker (41, below) ran a kickoff back a record 98 yards for a touchdown to put Miami ahead 17-10 at the half. But, as the sun was going down, Washington running back John Riggins (44) rose to the occasion, breaking through the compressed left side of the Dolphins' defense (opposite) in the fourth quarter for 43 yards, a touchdown, and, yes, another record.

Players and Coaches

"Fame! I'm gonna live forever." So go the words of the song. Nice lively beat. Nice ambitious sentiment. But "forever"? That depends; there are many kinds of fame.

There's celebrity, of the klieg light, theater marquee, magazine cover variety. There's prominence, of the political caucus, chairman of the board, honorary degree sort. Then there's the kind of fame accorded Super Bowl players and coaches, which is neither celebrity nor prominence but a little bit of both. It's difficult not to garner some measure of fame when you've been in a sporting event viewed by more than 100 million people around the world.

The coaches may be the most famous, if the term is taken to mean recognizable. Everybody knows them, their expressions, their quirks. After all, there have only been 18 of them, as exclusive a club as you'll find. They get the closeups; stoney-faced, nattily dressed, with game plans neatly rolled like the morning newspaper, or faces contorted, shouting, arms waving in shirtsleeves.

For the players, fame is distributed less equitably—more to the star quarterback seen as frequently in Broadway nightspots as in stadiums, less to journeymen as familiar with sitting on tractors in the offseason as on the bench.

But the winners all wear the same rings whether they were the most sought after postgame interviews or got less air time than a final guest on the "Tonight Show." And the losers all share a fierce desire to return. On either end of the score the Super Bowl is "it" in their world and they have been a part of "it." The game rubs off and sticks to the whorls of personality like gold dust on moistened fingertips.

True, for most players—winners and losers—the spheres of Super Bowl fame shrink as the game's Roman numerals climb. But as long as the game goes on and even after, their fame, of whatever magnitude, is assured.

It isn't the fame that matters, anyway, or living forever. To Super Bowl players and coaches what matters most is to have been there and, more important, to have won.

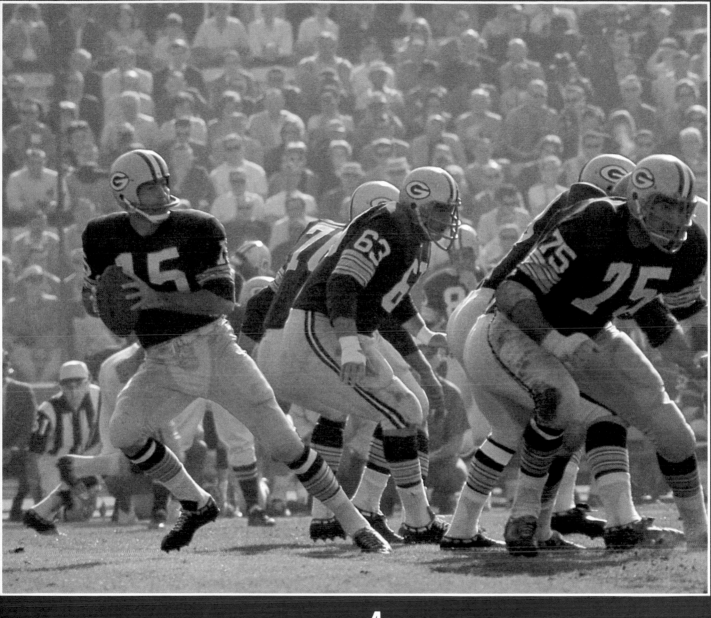

A study in bridled intensity, head coach Vince Lombardi (left) looks on as his Green Bay team performs up to his exacting expectations. The performance of Packers quarterback Bart Starr (15, above) was beyond reproach even to Lombardi's critical eye; he was named the most valuable player of the first two AFL-NFL World Championship Games.

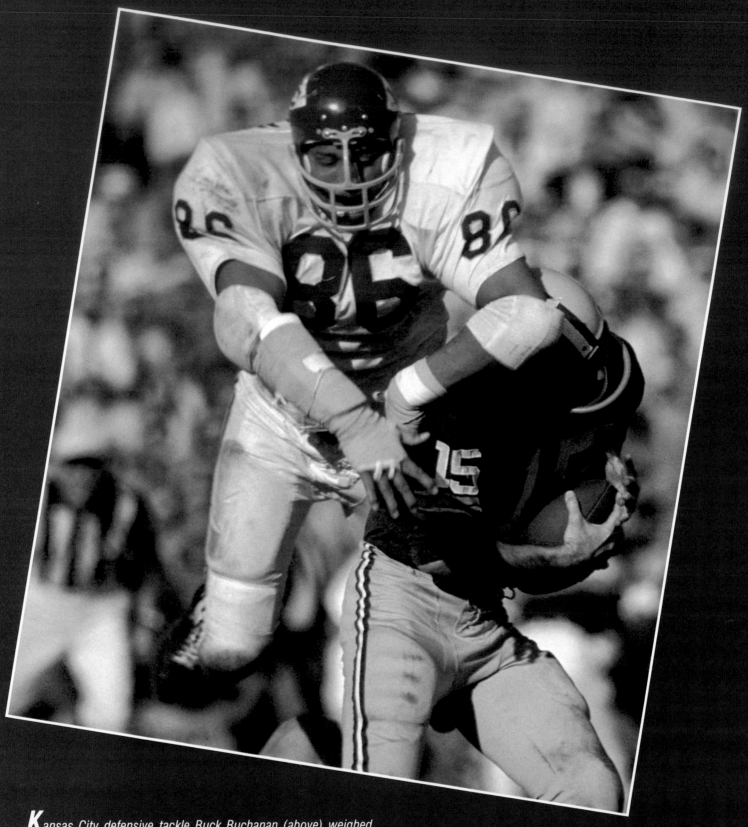

*K*ansas City defensive tackle Buck Buchanan (above) weighed heavily on Green Bay's Starr in Game I, just as the close halftime score—14-10 in favor of the Packers—weighed heavily upon NFL stalwarts. But from the beginning of the second half of that game through all four quarters of the next, one year later, the Super Bowl was the province of the Packers. Green Bay zeroed in on both titles the way defensive end Willie Davis (87, right) did on Raiders running back Hewritt Dixon (35) in Game II.

*L*ooking back on Super Bowl III, New York Jets middle line-backer Al Atkinson observed, "The Colts didn't have a psychological edge, not with Joe [Namath, 12, left] around. They knew we weren't gonna drop over in a faint when they walked on the field. We were a loose, cocky bunch. They were the big favorites but, mentally, I think we had the upper hand." Along with the odds, the Colts also had multi-talented running back Tom Matte (41, above) in their favor. He gained 116 yards on 11 carries and caught two passes for 30 more in the losing effort.

*P*laying in the heat of the Super Bowl spotlight, quarterbacks, in particular, can get burned. The Chiefs' Len Dawson (above) stayed cool in its glare at Game IV. Baltimore's Earl Morrall took heat of a different kind for the Colts' loss in Game III. But in Super Bowl V (right), when veteran Johnny Unitas was injured, Morrall made the most of the opportunity to redeem himself.

The powerhouse Dallas Cowboys team that rolled over Miami in Super Bowl VI also was a team with powerful internal contrasts. The most obvious involved the attitudes of two of the team's stars: aloof, enigmatic running back Duane Thomas (left) and consummate professional, defensive tackle Bob Lilly (sacking Miami's Bob Griese, above). Despite their differences, both Thomas and Lilly had tremendous games against the Dolphins.

*T*ackle Manny Fernandez (opposite) was the enforcer of Miami's No Name Defense in Super Bowl VII. Washington running back Larry Brown (left), the NFC's leading rusher that 1972 season, often was the enforcee. Although Brown gained 72 yards rushing and 26 more receiving, he was rendered ineffectual by the opportunistic Dolphins. ''We controlled their running game pretty well,'' said Miami middle linebacker Nick Buoniconti. ''The Redskins lost because they couldn't control Manny.''

The Vikings got figuratively snowed-in two Januarys in a row. At Game VIII, Dolphins fullback Larry Csonka (opposite) plowed through the Vikings' defense. In Super Bowl IX, against the Steelers, quarterback Fran Tarkenton (left) scrambled not by design but out of necessity. Even icy instructions from coach Bud Grant (below) couldn't stop Minnesota from being buried the way Pittsburgh's Jack Lambert did receiver John Gilliam (bottom).

*T*here are dominant personalities on every team, but few players have exhibited the sheer dynamism that defensive tackle Joe Greene (left) and middle linebacker Jack Lambert (above) did with the Pittsburgh Steelers. Whether on the sidelines, in the locker room, or in the thick of the action of Games IX, X, XIII, and XIV, Greene and Lambert were the reinforcing ramrods of the Steelers' monumental four Super Bowl victories.

Pro football's "winningest" team made up for an earlier Super Bowl loss in a big way, behind some big men. The Raiders' offensive linemen (left) —guard Gene Upshaw (63), tackle Art Shell, center Dave Dalby, guard George Buehler, and tackle John Vella—display the Super Bowl XI trophy they helped win. The man they protected all afternoon, quarterback Ken Stabler (12, above) congratulates wide receivers Fred Biletnikoff, the game's most valuable player, and Cliff Branch (21).

*D*enver roared into Game XII on the strength of its two-fisted Orange Crush defense. Unfortunately for the thousands of Broncos supporters who painted the town of New Orleans orange during Super Bowl week, defensive end Lyle Alzado (77, above), linebackers Randy Gradishar (53) and Bob Swenson (51), and the rest of the crushers found they had both fists full dealing with Dallas's perennial 1,000-yard rusher Tony Dorsett (33) and the game plan of Cowboys head coach Tom Landry (right), one of the league's master innovators.

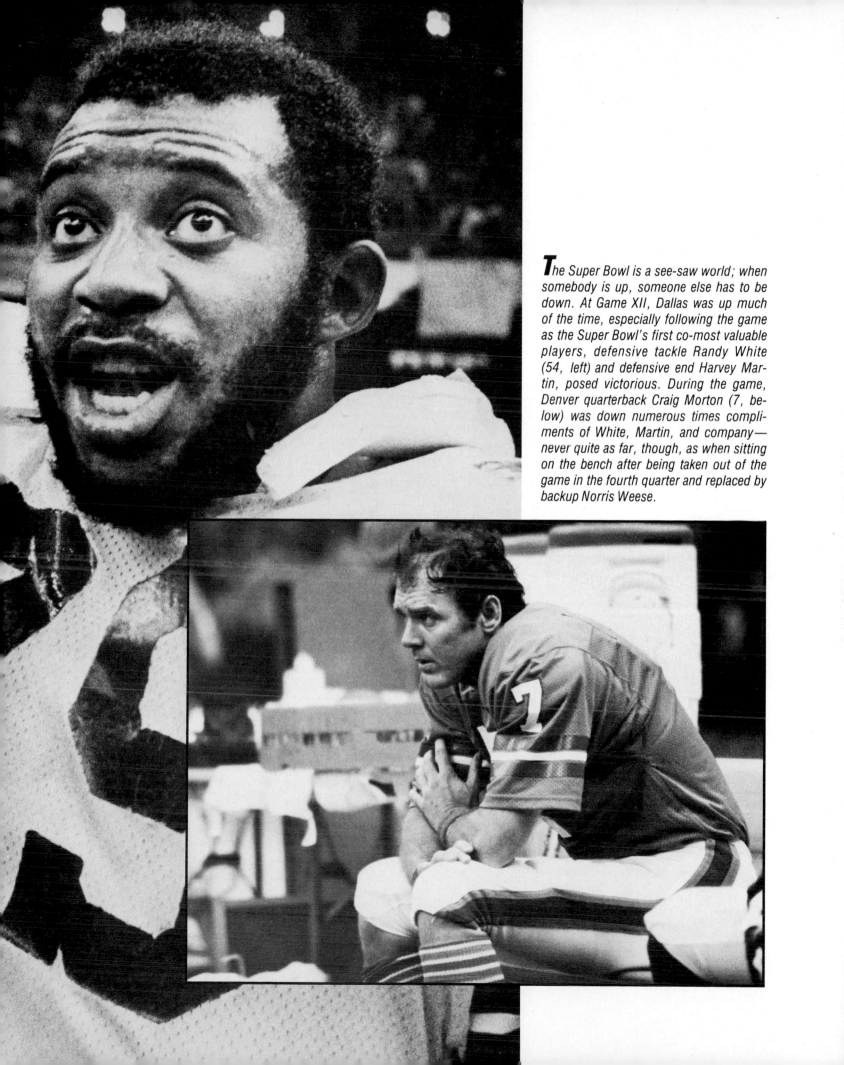

*T*he Super Bowl is a see-saw world; when somebody is up, someone else has to be down. At Game XII, Dallas was up much of the time, especially following the game as the Super Bowl's first co-most valuable players, defensive tackle Randy White (54, left) and defensive end Harvey Martin, posed victorious. During the game, Denver quarterback Craig Morton (7, below) was down numerous times compliments of White, Martin, and company— never quite as far, though, as when sitting on the bench after being taken out of the game in the fourth quarter and replaced by backup Norris Weese.

In one of the Super Bowl's most memorable acts of individual courage, defensive end Jack Youngblood (85, opposite) of the Los Angeles Rams played game XIV on a broken leg. His fierce determination characterized the entire Rams team as it went to the wall with the Steelers. Pittsburgh quarterback Terry Bradshaw (12, below), severely tested under fire in the previous Super Bowl, got hot in the second half against Los Angeles, connecting with stellar wide receiver John Stallworth (left) on two devastating bombs in the fourth quarter.

Quarterback Jim Plunkett (16, right, with safety Burgess Owens) was the comeback story of the year in 1980. Plunkett, a Heisman Trophy winner, was the number-one pick in the 1971 NFL draft, yet his career with New England, San Francisco, and Oakland had more ups and downs than the rides at Disneyland. When Raiders starting quarterback Dan Pastorini was injured in the fourth game of the 1980 season, Plunkett rose meteorically from the bench to become Super Bowl XV's most valuable player. In the locker room following the victory, head coach Tom Flores (opposite), once a Raiders quarterback himself, told his team something it already knew—the Raiders were number one.

To play superbly and win a Super Bowl is deserved. To play superbly and lose is the stuff of tragedy, as Cincinnati quarterback Ken Anderson (14, left) discovered at Super Bowl XVI. Anderson ran for one touchdown, threw for two more, and set a Super Bowl record for highest completion percentage (25 of 34, 73.5 percent), only to see San Francisco win. For the Bengals, the rub came in the third quarter when the 49ers' defense stopped them on the goal line. The big play of the dramatic series—and perhaps the play of the game—was linebacker Dan Bunz's crushing, touchdown-saving, third-down tackle (sequence) of running back Charles Alexander.

*L*inebacker Jack Reynolds (above) and guard Bob Kuechenberg (right) have played in six Super Bowls between them. Reynolds played in Game XIV with the Rams, and was lucky enough, in retrospect, to be acquired by San Francisco in time to go to Game XVI. There, he lent his spirited leadership and postseason experience to the 49ers' young defense, acting as an extra coach on and off the field. Kuechenberg, the epitome of the veteran trench warrior, has played his entire career with the Dolphins. He was one of only two players remaining from Miami's dynasty teams of Super Bowls VI, VII, and VIII to play in Game XVII (Vern Den Herder was the other).

*H*uman dynamo running back John Riggins of Washington turned in a performance at Super Bowl XVII that echoed those of Larry Csonka in Game VIII and Franco Harris in Game IX. Colorful, unpredictable, and quirky, Riggins (whose wardrobe prompted the comment, "He dresses like he lives in a duck blind") camped it up at a Super Bowl week party in top hat, white tie, and tails. But he was all business during the game, gaining 108 yards in the second half and a record 166 overall on 38 carries. Riggins also ran off with the most valuable player award.

S i d e l i n e s

Balloons, bands, guest stars, and singing groups; let's face it, the sports business is show business. A unique branch, perhaps, but show biz all the same. It thrives on the same sorts of drama and spectacle, climax and denouement, personalities and gimmicks as *Evita, Star Wars,* or "Hill Street Blues."

And sport's reigning show of shows is the Super Bowl.

While some may grouse that the game has become simply another television spectacular, an overblown annual network special that is better viewed at home where instant replay and cold beer are more easily available, for the relatively few football fans who ever have attended a Super Bowl game, the experience rates far beyond the realm of media hype and public relations hoopla.

In person, the game takes on a different feel, charged by the electricity of a crowd that knows it's at the only game not just in town, but America and, increasingly, the world that given Sunday in January. It's like attending a cross between Carnival in Rio, Macy's Thanksgiving Day parade, and St. Patrick's Day in Boston or Chicago with touches of *A Chorus Line,* the Academy Awards show, and a James Bond film thrown in for good measure.

Playing the game is the focus of it all, the reason the happening is happening. But when the game action stops, the show must go on.

*T*he fireworks at Super Bowl XIV were not confined to halftime, as the Pittsburgh Steelers pulled out a hard-fought victory over the Los Angeles Rams. The Steelers' victory over the Dallas Cowboys in the previous game is remembered as one of the most exciting Super Bowls of all, one made even more memorable by the presence of league patriarch George Halas, who arrived in a vintage automobile to toss the coin at the pregame ceremonies.

XIV

XV

More than 76,000 people, captivated by the action at Game XV, the glitter of the Raiders' cheerleaders, and a Mardi Gras halftime, helped pay symbolic tribute to the 52 Americans who had been held captive in Iran. An enormous yellow ribbon, reflecting the welcome home sentiment of the song "Tie a Yellow Ribbon," hung on the Louisiana Superdome, while the Raiders and Eagles players wore yellow tape on the backs of their helmets.

Going to the Super Bowl may be an out-of-this-world occasion, but it's down-to-earth compared to the lunar exploits of the Apollo 8 astronauts who attended Game III in Miami, the first officially titled "Super Bowl." At Super Bowl VII NASA played a return engagement, sending the crew and re-entry-blackened capsule back from the Apollo 16 mission as an added sideline attraction.

III

X

An old regular at the Super Bowl became a new star in Hollywood: the Goodyear Blimp. Using Game X as a backdrop and the crowd of 80,187 as extras, the climactic scene of the movie Black Sunday was filmed on location at the Orange Bowl. Sharing top billing with a blimp was a first for the film's principals, who included the late Robert Shaw and director John Frankenheimer (far left).

Hot halftime hues augmented the already heated play of the Miami Dolphins and Washington Redskins at Super Bowl XVII. The Rose Bowl was literally filled with living color, as more than 100,000 fans participated in a spectacular stadium card stunt. The previous year, at the Pontiac Silverdome, Diana Ross didn't sing "Baby, It's Cold Outside" even though prompted by sub-freezing temperatures. She sang the National Anthem instead.

XVI

127

IV

A pregame balloon stunt turned unexpectedly into an audience participation event at Game IV. Two hot air balloons, one containing a rider dressed as a Viking, the other an Indian chief, were to be launched. The Vikings' balloon broke loose from its moorings, sailed across the field, caught on a loud speaker pole, and crashed into the field-level seats in the end zone of Tulane Stadium. No one was injured. The Chiefs' balloon never took off—unlike the Bourbon Street stripper at Game IX, who nearly took it all off.

IX

The city of Pittsburgh, after waiting 42 years for its first NFL title, suddenly became the city of champions in the late 1970s. The Steelers won back-to-back Super Bowls (IX and X) then sandwiched a Pirates' 1979 World Series victory between Super Bowl wins in Games XIII and XIV. The men of the hour at Super Bowl XIV were Pirates first baseman Willie Stargell and Steelers quarterback Terry Bradshaw; the talisman of the hour was a waving towel called ''terrible'' by thousand of Steelers fans.

XIV

The Super Bowl has become as much a media event as a sporting event. Every year more press credentials are requested; nearly 2,000 were issued for Game XVII in Pasadena to media representatives from all over America and dozens of foreign countries. Most of the working journalists attend the press conference held on the Friday before each game. At Super Bowl XV in New Orleans, Commissioner Pete Rozelle fielded questions, then posed with the 23 media members who had covered all 15 games to date.

Game XIII was a gem, as was its Caribbean halftime (overleaf), which lit the Orange Bowl like a jewel against the Miami dusk.

XIII

E m o t i o n s

The Super Bowl. To get there, you do all you can and what you must. To win there, you do more.

"We're proud to come to Los Angeles 16-0," said Miami Dolphins head coach Don Shula before Game VII. "But we still have to win the Super Bowl. This is a game we've worked for all year. How good a team we really are will be determined by the outcome of the Super Bowl."

The Dolphins triumphed. However, they knew all along that there was much more riding on the final score than a perfect record.

"The funny thing about this game," Miami defensive tackle Manny Fernandez reflected later, "is that we came in here 16-0 and if we would have lost we would have been the biggest bunch of ----- in the world."

Such is the nature of the Super Bowl. When you win, you win it all. When you lose, you lose everything.

"It doesn't do any good to play in the Super Bowl if you don't win," said Washington head coach George Allen after Game VII.

"Anyone who says one loss cannot ruin a season never lost a Super Bowl," said Philadelphia head coach Dick Vermeil after Game XV.

"When you walk out on the field for this game," said Cincinnati's Super Bowl XVI quarterback, Ken Anderson, "it's the greatest feeling in the world. And when you walk off, and you haven't won, it's the worst feeling in the world."

The Super Bowl. It is the reason to endure the heat and punishment of training camp two-a-days. It is balm for six months of aching. It is compensation for the hours of films and meetings and playbooks.

But what about the money? Isn't the money as big an incentive as the game?

"The money?" mused winning Super Bowl XVII quarterback Joe Theismann of Washington. "The money's great. But, look, the money's gonna be gone. I mean, if I don't spend it, my wife will. But the ring. . .the ring is mine forever."

The Super Bowl. You don't win it for money. You win it because you may never get a chance to win it again.

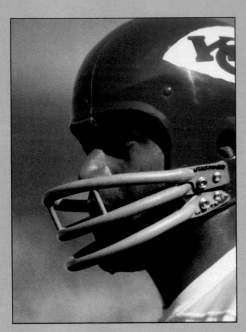

The first championship meeting of the rival AFL and NFL prompted plenty of speculation, little of it from the players involved. Except, that is, Kansas City cornerback Fred Williamson (above), who promised to personally hammer the Packers. As the game waned, and Green Bay guard Fuzzy Thurston (63) and running back Elijah Pitts (right) sensed victory, pregame threats echoed as hollow boasts.

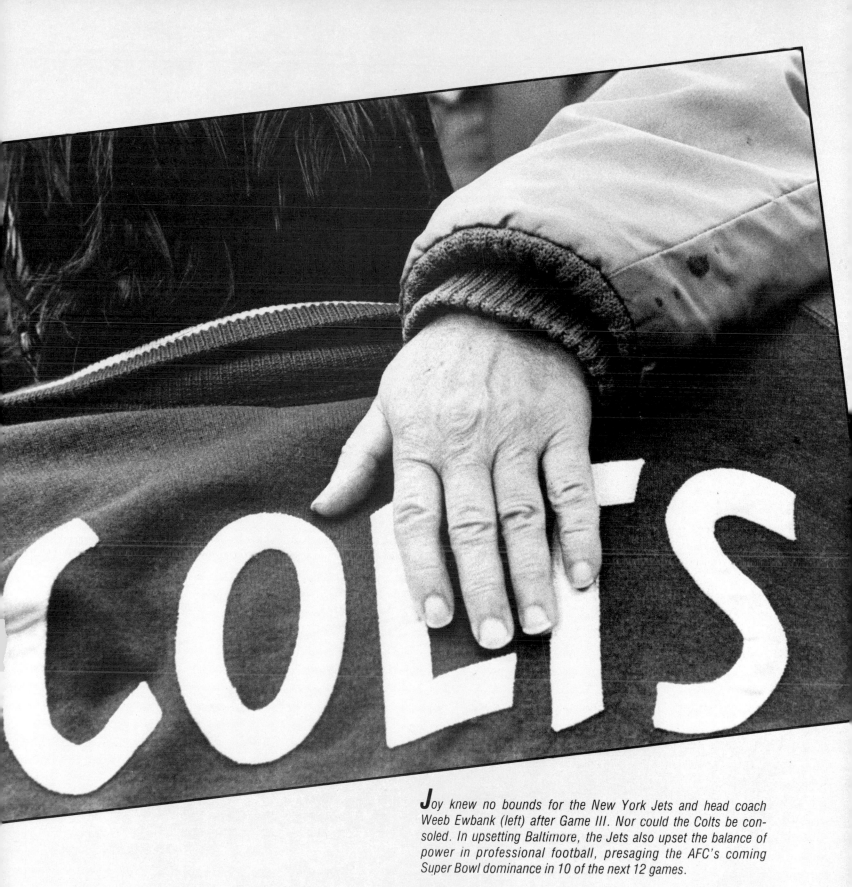

*J*oy knew no bounds for the New York Jets and head coach Weeb Ewbank (left) after Game III. Nor could the Colts be consoled. In upsetting Baltimore, the Jets also upset the balance of power in professional football, presaging the AFC's coming Super Bowl dominance in 10 of the next 12 games.

The pain of the moment ebbed for feisty Minnesota quarterback Joe Kapp; the pain of losing Game IV did not. His desperation third-quarter scoring drive was neutralized on the succeeding series by a 46-yard touchdown pass to Kansas City wide receiver Otis Taylor (89, below). The exultation he shared with running back Mike Garrett was reflected in the face of Chiefs head coach Hank Stram (overleaf), afloat on a sea of his reveling players.

*S*uper Bowl V and VI are inevitably linked, a splendid example of cause and effect at work. Jim O'Brien's last-second field goal (below) vindicated the Colts in Super Bowl play. But the successful kick prompted disgruntled Dallas defensive tackle Bob Lilly (74, right) to heave his helmet far downfield as the victorious Colts strode to the sidelines. Lilly's anger was the spark that ignited the Cowboys' inexorable drive to Game VI the next season.

*G*ame V, like all Super Bowls, produced highs and lows in equal measure. Baltimore's Johnny Unitas (19), one of the game's greatest quarterbacks, played sparingly in Super Bowl III because of a sore passing arm. He was expected to star in Game V, but was brought to his knees (left) in the first quarter by defensive end George Andrie's (66) jarring tackle. Unitas was forced to leave the field with injured ribs and did not return. Late in the game, Dan Reeves's (30) muffed pass reception was intercepted, and led to the Colts' winning field goal. The dejected Reeves (above) had to suffer the jeering congratulations of the celebrating Colts as he pushed his way to the sidelines.

A perfect season. The odds against it happening were staggering. Needless to say, it did happen, though even after Super Bowl VII, amidst clicking cameras and cheering supporters, Miami head coach Don Shula (above) looked as if he still didn't believe the "ultimate" dream had come true. Washington running back Larry Brown (left) believed it. His Super Bowl dream was gone.

*B*ill Arnsparger (above), the defensive architect of the Dolphins' dynasty, can't contain his bittersweet tears after Miami's second straight Super Bowl victory in Game VIII. On his way to the locker room, he is hugged by long-time coaching associate and friend, Don Shula, whom Arnsparger would be leaving after being named head coach of the New York Giants. Arnsparger had previously been the defensive line coach under Shula at Baltimore for six years, and was the first assistant coach Shula named in 1970 when he moved to Miami.

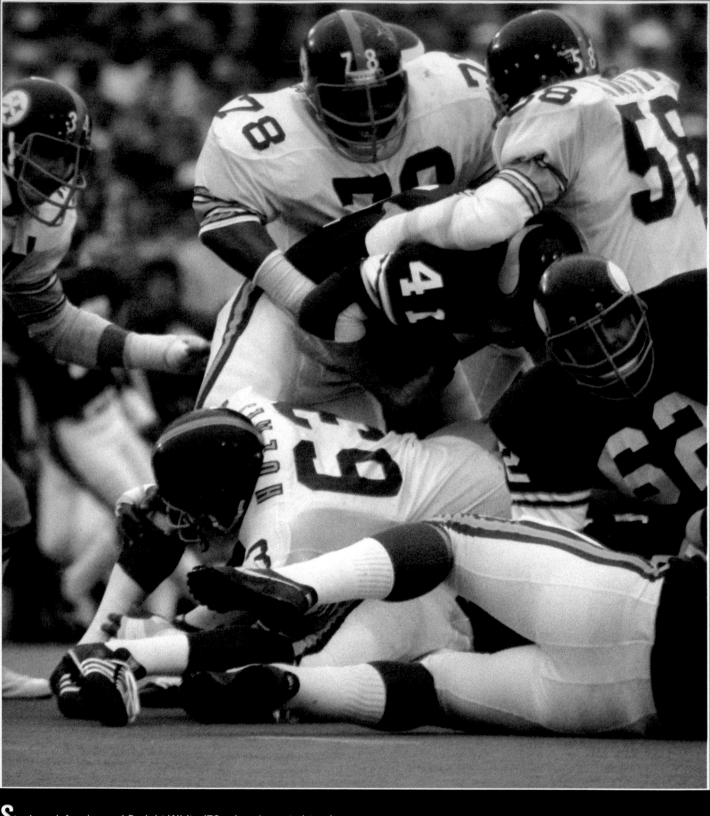

Steelers defensive end Dwight White (78, above) wanted to play in Super Bowl IX in the worst way, and nothing, not even being hospitalized twice before the game with a viral infection, or the best efforts of the Vikings' offensive line, was going to stop him. "Dwight spread germs," said defensive linemate Joe Greene. "The rest of us spread fear." The next year, at Game X, fearsome linebacker Jack Lambert (right) spread himself around, intimidating the Cowboys from sideline to sideline.

Doubt began creeping into Minnesota's game plan as early as the first quarter of Game XI. Verging on what would have been only their third Super Bowl offensive touchdown in four games, the Vikings fumbled the ball away at the 3 yard line. Oakland linebacker Willie Hall (39, above) made sure the turnover didn't escape the disgusted Fran Tarkenton's notice. At Game XII, defensive end Harvey Martin (right) erased any doubts as to who was number one after the Cowboys' victory.

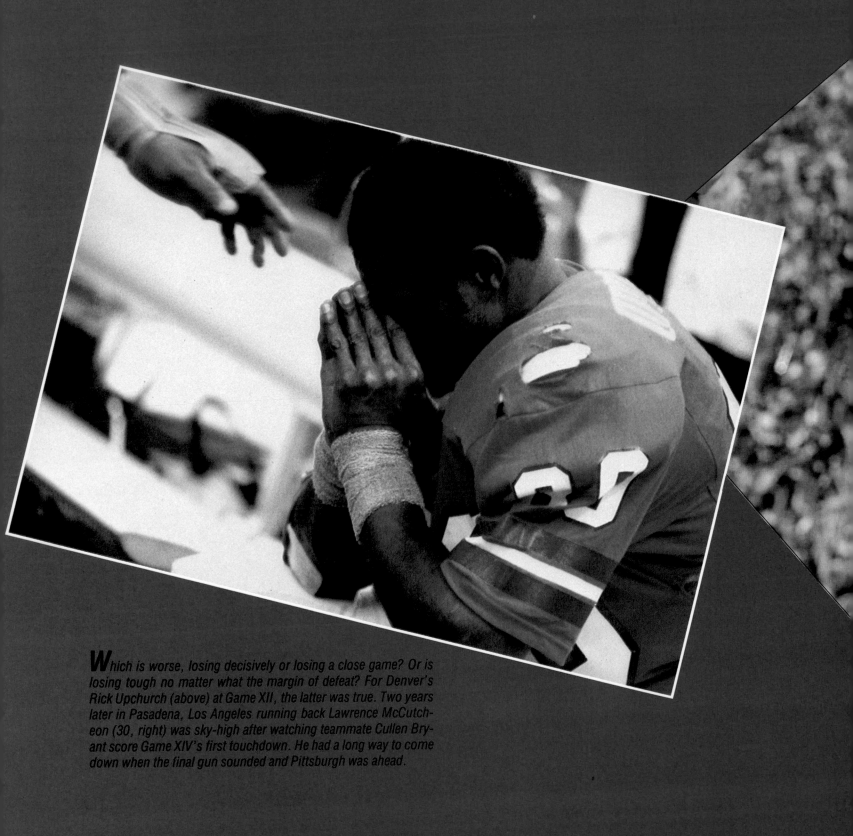

Which is worse, losing decisively or losing a close game? Or is losing tough no matter what the margin of defeat? For Denver's Rick Upchurch (above) at Game XII, the latter was true. Two years later in Pasadena, Los Angeles running back Lawrence McCutcheon (30, right) was sky-high after watching teammate Cullen Bryant score Game XIV's first touchdown. He had a long way to come down when the final gun sounded and Pittsburgh was ahead.

*F*ootball is a sport, not a war. Yet the words of General George S. Patton underline the success of the Steelers. "It is the spirit of the men who follow," wrote Patton, "and of the man who leads that gains the victory." At Super Bowl XIV, the Steelers staged a spirited celebration following Franco Harris's (32, left) touch-down, which iced the game late in the fourth quarter. Once the locker room salvos had subsided, head coach Chuck Noll (above), the man who led Pittsburgh to four Super Bowl victories, stopped to savor the sweet, fleeting moment.

The Cinderella hero of a wild card team, Raiders quarterback Jim Plunkett (16, right) drew a crowd after Super Bowl XV, including Eagles head coach Dick Vermeil, who congratulated the big quarterback on his team's victory. Defensive end Claude Humphrey (below, throwing an official's flag after being called for roughing the passer) was one of a crowd of frustrated Eagles who wanted to get to Plunkett all evening, but couldn't.

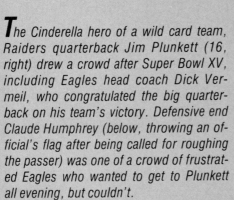

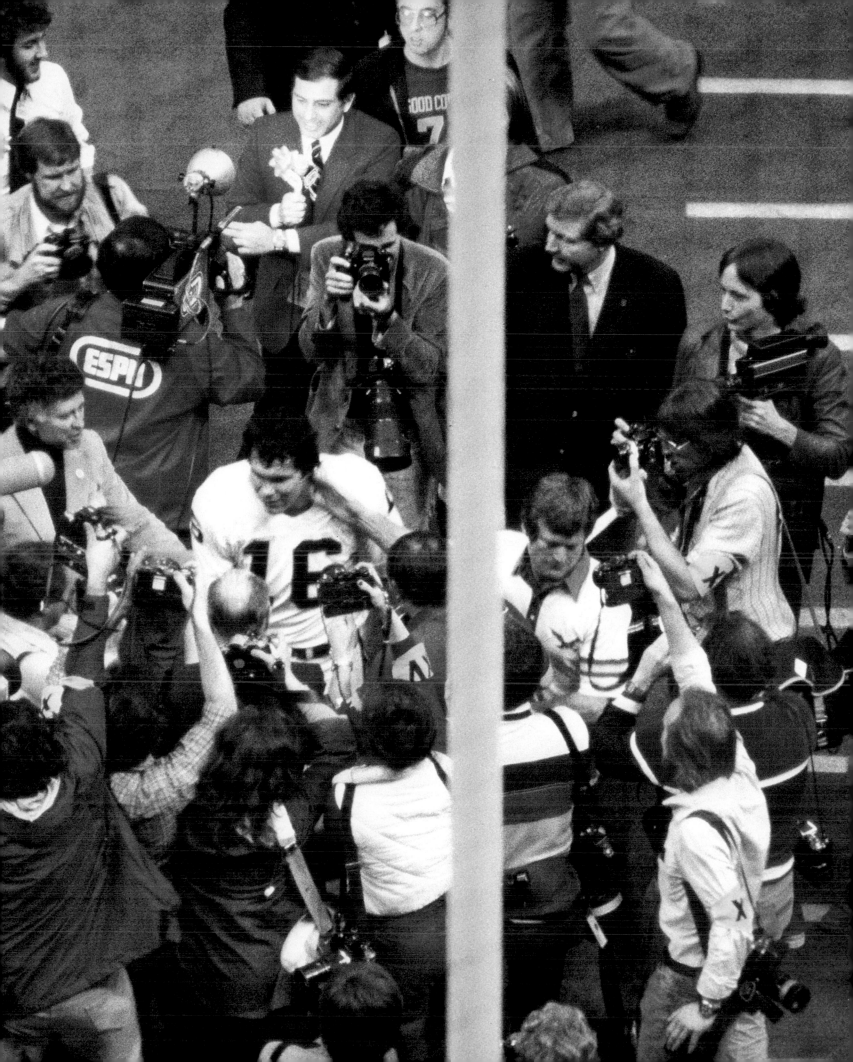

Winners rejoice. Losers long to be winners. It's as simple as that. At Game XV, the Raiders, including rookie linebacker Matt Millen (55, opposite) and nose tackle Reggie Kinlaw, rejoiced. On the other side of the Louisiana Superdome, the longing looks belonged to the Eagles, especially rookie cornerback Roynell Young (left). Young had spent the game covering Cliff Branch, who caught two touchdown passes.

*T*ime after time a game turns on one crucial play or one critical series. For some games it's difficult to pinpoint them exactly. For other games, such as Super Bowl XVI, it's not hard at all; that game hinged on the 49ers' defensive unit's magnificent goal-line stand late in the third quarter. Though nose tackle Archie Reese (78, right) was perhaps most prominent in the fourth-down pileup, the official play-by-play statistical sheet credited the tackle to "entire middle of line."

*E*ven without the tiger stripes it's a jungle out there on the Super Bowl field as two rookies—Bengals wide receiver Cris Collinsworth and 49ers cornerback Eric Wright (above)—discover in Game XVI. Collinsworth held on to the pass for a 49-yard gain, one of a number of big plays that rallied Cincinnati in the second half. However, San Francisco held on to the lead that Randy Cross (51, right), Archie Reese (78), and their exuberant teammates took into the locker room at the half.

There are as many styles of marking a Super Bowl touchdown as there are players who have scored. Opposite extremes were represented by Washington Redskins teammates Charlie Brown and John Riggins at Game XVII. Wide receiver Brown chose a leaping, ball twirling end zone spike. Running back Riggins took it in stride, a workman going home, the job done.

Appendix

Super Bowl I

Green Bay 35, Kansas City 10

There was no shortage of talk before the First AFL-NFL Championship Game. But when January 15 of 1967 finally came, the talk ceased; it was time for football's biggest showdown.

The Green Bay Packers would carry the 47-year-old shield of the established, entrenched National Football League against the Kansas City Chiefs, champions of the seven-year-old American Football League.

Tom Catlin, defensive coach for the Los Angeles Rams, was in a position to know about this first matchup. The previous season he had been defensive coach for the Chiefs.

"I don't expect Kansas City to win," he said, "but it's not at all impossible that they might. They would have to play an almost perfect game and the Green Bay defense creates situations in which you make mistakes."

In the first half, the Packers, playing without injured running back Paul Hornung and receiver Boyd Dowler, sparred and probed. Their probing brought them 14 points, but their defense seemed confused on how to contain Kansas City's moving pocket.

Members of the NFL establishment wore looks of worry at the halftime break. But, in the Green Bay locker room, coach Vince Lombardi was about to activate the Packers' warhead.

The explosion was set off by a defensive tactic that Lombardi had always scorned: the blitz. In this case it was a two-man attack that rattled Len Dawson, the Chiefs' quarterback.

Dawson, hurried and bumped on a third-quarter pass, failed to see Packers safety Willie Wood hovering near tight end Fred Arbanas, the intended receiver. Wood intercepted the pass and returned it 50 yards to set up a touchdown by Elijah Pitts.

Minutes later, Green Bay had the ball again. Bart Starr passed three times to veteran Max McGee and the Packers had their fourth touchdown—and, later, the game 35-10. Starr was named most valuable player, but McGee was most valuable receiver with seven catches for 138 yards.

Participants—Kansas City Chiefs, champions of the American Football League, and Green Bay Packers, champions of the National Football League

Date—January 15, 1967

Site—Los Angeles Memorial Coliseum

Time—1:05 P.M. PST

Conditions—72 degrees, sunny

Playing Surface—Grass

Television and Radio—National Broadcasting Company (NBC) and Columbia Broadcasting System (CBS)

Regular Season Records—Kansas City, 11-2-1; Green Bay, 12-2

League Championships—Kansas City defeated the Buffalo Bills 31-7 for the AFL title; Green Bay defeated the Dallas Cowboys 34-27 for the NFL title

Players' Shares—$15,000 to each member of the winning team; $7,500 to each member of the losing team

Attendance—61,946

Gross Receipts—$2,768,211.64

Officials—Referee, Norm Schachter, NFL; umpire, George Young, AFL; line judge, Al Sabato, AFL; head linesman, Bernie Ulman, NFL; back judge, Jack Reader, AFL; field judge, Mike Lisetski, NFL.

Coaches—Hank Stram, Kansas City; Vince Lombardi, Green Bay

Blitzes—and defensive end Willie Davis (87)—hurried Chiefs quarterback Len Dawson.

Kansas City	Starters, Offense	Green Bay
Chris Burford	WR	Carroll Dale
Jim Tyrer	LT	Bob Skoronski
Ed Budde	LG	Fred (Fuzzy) Thurston
Wayne Frazier	C	Bill Curry
Curt Merz	RG	Jerry Kramer
Dave Hill	RT	Forrest Gregg
Fred Arbanas	TE	Marv Fleming
Otis Taylor	WR	Boyd Dowler
Len Dawson	QB	Bart Starr
Mike Garrett	RB	Elijah Pitts
Curtis McClinton	RB	Jim Taylor
	Starters, Defense	
Jerry Mays	LE	Willie Davis
Andy Rice	LT	Ron Kostelnik
Buck Buchanan	RT	Henry Jordan
Chuck Hurston	RE	Lionel Aldridge
Bobby Bell	LLB	Dave Robinson
Sherrill Headrick	MLB	Ray Nitschke
E. J. Holub	RLB	Lee Roy Caffey
Fred Williamson	LCB	Herb Adderley
Willie Mitchell	RCB	Bob Jeter
Bobby Hunt	LS	Tom Brown
Johnny Robinson	RS	Willie Wood

Kansas City	0	10	0	0	—	10
Green Bay	7	7	14	7	—	35

GB—McGee 37 pass from Starr (Chandler kick)
KC—McClinton 7 pass from Dawson (Mercer kick)
GB—Taylor 14 run (Chandler kick)
KC—FG Mercer 31
GB—Pitts 5 run (Chandler kick)
GB—McGee 13 pass from Starr (Chandler kick)
GB—Pitts 1 run (Chandler kick)

TEAM STATISTICS	KC	GB
First downs	17	21
Rushing	4	10
Passing	12	11
By penalty	1	0
Total yardage	239	358
Net rushing yardage	72	130
Net passing yardage	167	228
Passes att.-comp.-had int.	32-17-1	24-16-1

RUSHING

Kansas City—Dawson, 3 for 24; Garrett, 6 for 17; McClinton, 6 for 16; Beathard, 1 for 14; Coan, 3 for 1.

Green Bay—J. Taylor, 16 for 53; 1 TD; Pitts, 11 for 45, 2 TDs; D. Anderson, 4 for 30; Grabowski, 2 for 2.

PASSING

Kansas City—Dawson, 16 of 27 for 211, 1 TD, 1 int.; Beathard, 1 of 5 for 17.

Green Bay—Starr, 16 of 23 for 250, 2 TDs, 1 int.; Bratkowski, 0 of 1.

RECEIVING

Kansas City—Burford, 4 for 67; O. Taylor, 4 for 57; Garrett, 3 for 28; McClinton, 2 for 34, 1 TD; Arbanas, 2 for 30; Carolan, 1 for 7; Coan, 1 for 5.

Green Bay—McGee, 7 for 138, 2 TDs; Dale, 4 for 59; Pitts, 2 for 32; Fleming, 2 for 22; J. Taylor, 1 for -1.

PUNTING

Kansas City—Wilson, 7 for 317, 45.3 average.

Green Bay—Chandler, 3 for 130, 43.3 average; D. Anderson, 1 for 43.

PUNT RETURNS

Kansas City—Garrett, 2 for 17; E. Thomas, 1 for 2.

Green Bay—D. Anderson, 3 for 25; Wood, 1 for -2, 1 fair catch.

KICKOFF RETURNS

Kansas City—Coan, 4 for 87; Garrett, 2 for 23.

Green Bay—Adderley, 2 for 40; D. Anderson, 1 for 25.

INTERCEPTIONS

Kansas City—Mitchell, 1 for 0.

Green Bay—Wood, 1 for 50.

Super Bowl II
Green Bay 33, Oakland 14

The rumors had circulated around the NFL for weeks: Vince Lombardi was returning to his native New York to coach the Jets. Or, he was accepting the challenge of rebuilding the Chicago Bears. Or, he was easing off, moving full time to the front office.

One thing seemed certain, though. The second Super Bowl would be his last game as head coach of the Packers. An era—in Green Bay and the NFL—was drawing to a close.

Lombardi made it semi-official to his players two days before their game with the Oakland Raiders, telling them during a meeting, "It may be the last time we are all together."

If the Raiders were mismatched against the Packers, as some contended, their handicap would be enormous now that the Green Bay veterans, the men who had been with Lombardi from the start, saw the game as one giant going-away party for Lombardi.

What a celebration they made it!

Green Bay scored on its first three possessions. Don Chandler kicked a 39-yard field goal, and then a 20-yarder after an eight-minute drive that began at the Packers' 3-yard line.

The third score was a thunderbolt. After punting the ball away, Oakland decided to blitz on first down. Starr's primary target, Carroll Dale, was covered closely by Willie Brown, but safety Howie Williams failed to pick up Boyd Dowler from cornerback Kent McCloughan; Starr lofted a pass to Dowler for a 62-yard touchdown.

"Bart Starr," Raiders defensive tackle Tom Keating was to marvel later, "reads a 'dog' better than any man I've ever seen."

The Raiders came back to score a touchdown pass on Daryle Lamonica's 23-yard pass to Bill Miller. But Starr's bomb had shaken the young AFL team. Linebacker Dan Conners stopped Travis Williams of the Packers on third down at the Green Bay 16, but Oakland's Rodger Bird muffed the punt return and Dick Capp recovered for the Packers.

Chandler's subsequent 43-yard field goal and Herb Adderley's fourth-quarter 60-yard interception return for a score assured the success of the farewell party.

Participants—Oakland Raiders, champions of the American Football League, and Green Bay Packers, champions of the National Football League
Date—January 14, 1968
Site—Orange Bowl, Miami
Time—3:05 P.M. EST
Conditions—86, partly cloudy
Playing Surface—Grass
Television and Radio—Columbia Broadcasting System (CBS)
Regular Season Records—Oakland, 13-1, Green Bay, 9-4-1
League Championships—Oakland defeated the Houston Oilers 40-7 for the AFL title; Green Bay defeated the Dallas Cowboys 21-17 for the NFL title
Players' Shares—$15,000 to each member of the winning team; $7,500 to each member of the losing team
Attendance—75,546
Gross Receipts—$3,349,106.89
Officials—Referee, Jack Vest, AFL; umpire, Ralph Morcroft, NFL; line judge, Bruce Alford, NFL; head linesman, Tony Veteri, AFL; back judge, Stan Javie, NFL; field judge, Bob Bauer, AFL
Coaches—John Rauch, Oakland; Vince Lombardi, Green Bay

Forrest Gregg (left) and Jerry Kramer gave Vince Lombardi one last Packers victory ride.

Green Bay	Starters, Offense	Oakland
Boyd Dowler	WR	Bill Miller
Bob Skoronski	LT	Bob Svihus
Gale Gillingham	LG	Gene Upshaw
Ken Bowman	C	Jim Otto
Jerry Kramer	RG	Wayne Hawkins
Forrest Gregg	RT	Harry Schuh
Marv Fleming	TE	Billy Cannon
Carroll Dale	WR	Fred Biletnikoff
Bart Starr	QB	Daryle Lamonica
Donny Anderson	RB	Pete Banaszak
Ben Wilson	RB	Hewritt Dixon
	Starters, Defense	
Willie Davis	LE	Isaac Lassiter
Ron Kostelnik	LT	Dan Birdwell
Henry Jordan	RT	Tom Keating
Lionel Aldridge	RE	Ben Davidson
Dave Robinson	LLB	Bill Laskey
Ray Nitschke	MLB	Dan Conners
Lee Roy Caffey	RLB	Gus Otto
Herb Adderley	LCB	Kent McCloughan
Bob Jeter	RCB	Willie Brown
Tom Brown	LS	Warren Powers
Willie Wood	RS	Howie Williams

Green Bay	3	13	10	7	— 33
Oakland	0	7	0	7	— 14

GB —FG Chandler 39
GB —FG Chandler 20
GB —Dowler 62 pass from Starr (Chandler kick)
Oak—Miller 23 pass from Lamonica (Blanda kick)
GB —FG Chandler 43
GB —Anderson 2 run (Chandler kick)
GB —FG Chandler 31
GB —Adderley 60 interception return (Chandler kick)
Oak—Miller 23 pass from Lamonica (Blanda kick)

TEAM STATISTICS	GB	Oak
First downs	19	16
Rushing	11	5
Passing	7	10
By penalty	1	1
Total yardage	322	293
Net rushing yardage	160	107
Net passing yardage	162	186
Passes att.-comp.-had int.	24-13-0	34-15-1

RUSHING
Green Bay—Wilson, 17 for 62; Anderson, 14 for 48, 1 TD; Williams, 8 for 36; Starr, 1 for 14; Mercein, 1 for 0.
Oakland—Dixon, 12 for 54; Todd, 2 for 37; Banaszak, 6 for 16.
PASSING
Green Bay—Starr, 13 of 24 for 202, 1 TD.
Oakland—Lamonica, 15 for 34 for 208, 2 TDs, 1 int.
RECEIVING
Green Bay—Dale, 4 for 43; Fleming, 4 for 35; Dowler, 2 for 71, 1 TD; Anderson, 2 for 18; McGee, 1 for 35.
Oakland—Miller, 5 for 84, 2 TDs; Banaszak, 4 for 69; Cannon, 2 for 25; Biletnikoff, 2 for 10; Wells, 1 for 17; Dixon, 1 for 3.
PUNTING
Green Bay—Anderson, 6 for 234, 39.0 average.
Oakland—Eischeid, 6 for 264, 44.0 average.
PUNT RETURNS
Green Bay—Wood, 5 for 35.
Oakland—Bird, 2 for 12, 1 fair catch.
KICKOFF RETURNS
Green Bay—Adderley, 1 for 24; Williams, 1 for 18; Crutcher, 1 for 7.
Oakland—Todd, 3 for 63; Grayson, 2 for 61; Hawkins, 1 for 3; Kocourek, 1 for 0, Kocourek lateraled to Grayson, who returned 11 yards.
INTERCEPTIONS
Green Bay—Adderley, 1 for 60, 1 TD.
Oakland—None.

Super Bowl III

New York Jets 16, Baltimore 7

Lou Michaels, the pugnacious Baltimore defensive end and kicker, was relaxing in a Ft. Lauderdale bar several nights before Game III. His eyes scanned the room and found a dark-haired, sleepy-eyed man he knew only by reputation.

"Namath," said Michaels, approaching the table of the young Jets quarterback. "You been doing a lot of talking."

"Lot to talk about," answered Joe Namath. "We're going to kick the hell out of your team."

Michaels was nonplussed. Here was this wise guy Namath, not only saying that his Jets would beat the Colts, not only disparaging Baltimore quarterbacks Earl Morrall and Johnny Unitas, but, later (at a sports dinner at Miami Springs Villa the Thursday night before the game), actually guaranteeing victory in public.

The game started as if the guarantee could never be redeemed. The Colts drove deep into New York territory on their first possession, but came up short; Michaels missed a 27-yard field goal. The third time the Colts had the ball, Al Atkinson deflected Morrall's pass from the Jets' 6. It was intercepted by Randy Beverly.

The Jets suddenly were aroused, as was the crowd in the Orange Bowl. Namath confidently moved his team downfield. When Namath's pass to George Sauer gave New York a first down on the Colts' 23, the Baltimore defenders cursed themselves in frustration.

A played called "19 Option," with Matt Snell carrying four yards into the end zone, gave the AFL its first lead in Super Bowl history.

The Colts' poise deteriorated just before the half when Morrall failed to see an open Jimmy Orr in the end zone on a flea-flicker play and was intercepted by Jim Hudson.

The Colts fumbled on their first play of the second half. Nine downs later the Jets had a 10-0 lead on Jim Turner's 32-yard field goal. Turner kicked two more before Baltimore scored.

The game ended with the Jets 16-7 victors. Namath trotted off the field, forefinger raised signifying that, for the moment, he, the Jets, head coach Weeb Ewbank, and the AFL were all number one in professional football.

Participants—New York Jets, champions of the American Football League, and Baltimore Colts, champions of the National Football League
Date—January 12, 1969
Site—Orange Bowl, Miami
Time—3:05 P.M. EST
Conditions—73 degrees, overcast, threat of rain
Playing Surface—Grass
Television and Radio—National Broadcasting Company (NBC)
Regular Season Records—New York, 11-3; Baltimore, 13-1
League Championships—New York defeated the Oakland Raiders 27-23 for the AFL title; Baltimore defeated the Cleveland Browns 34-0 for the NFL title
Players' Shares—$15,000 to each member of the winning team; $7,500 to each member of the losing team
Attendance—75,377
Gross Receipts—$3,374,985.64
Officials—Referee, Tommy Bell, NFL; umpire, Walt Parker, AFL; line judge, Cal LePore, AFL; head linesman, George Murphy, NFL; back judge, Jack Reader, AFL; field judge, Joe Gonzales, NFL
Coaches—Weeb Ewbank, New York; Don Shula, Baltimore

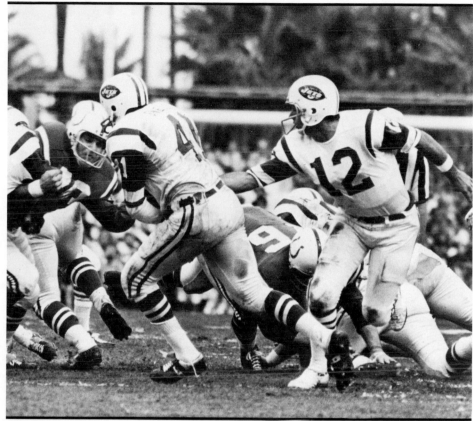

Matt Snell made no "guarantees," just yardage, much of it behind tackle Winston Hill.

N.Y. Jets	Starters, Offense	Baltimore
George Sauer	WR	Jimmy Orr
Winston Hill	LT	Bob Vogel
Bob Talamini	LG	Glenn Ressler
John Schmitt	C	Bill Curry
Randy Rasmussen	RG	Dan Sullivan
Dave Herman	RT	Sam Ball
Pete Lammons	TE	John Mackey
Don Maynard	WR	Willie Richardson
Joe Namath	QB	Earl Morrall
Emerson Boozer	RB	Tom Matte
Matt Snell	RB	Jerry Hill
	Starters, Defense	
Gerry Philbin	LE	Charles (Bubba) Smith
Paul Rochester	LT	Billy Ray Smith
John Elliott	RT	Fred Miller
Verlon Biggs	RE	Ordell Braase
Ralph Baker	LLB	Mike Curtis
Al Atkinson	MLB	Dennis Gaubatz
Larry Grantham	RLB	Don Shinnick
Johnny Sample	LCB	Bobby Boyd
Randy Beverly	RCB	Lenny Lyles
Jim Hudson	LS	Jerry Logan
Bill Baird	RS	Rick Volk

New York Jets	0	7	6	3	—	16
Baltimore	0	0	0	7	—	7

NYJ—Snell 4 run (Turner kick)
NYJ—FG Turner 32
NYJ—FG Turner 30
NYJ—FG Turner 9
Balt—Hill 1 run (Michaels kick)

TEAM STATISTICS	NYJ	Balt
First downs	21	18
Rushing	10	7
Passing	10	9
By penalty	1	2
Total yardage	337	324
Net rushing yardage	142	143
Net passing yardage	195	181
Passes att.-comp.-had int.	29-17-0	41-17-4

RUSHING
New York Jets—Snell, 30 for 121, 1 TD; Boozer, 10 for 19; Mathis, 3 for 2.
Baltimore—Matte, 11 for 116; Hill, 9 for 29, 1 TD; Unitas, 1 for 0; Morrall, 2 for -2.

PASSING
New York Jets—Namath, 17 of 28 for 206; Parilli, 0 of 1.
Baltimore—Morrall, 6 of 17 for 71, 3 int.; Unitas, 11 of 24 for 110, 1 int.

RECEIVING
New York Jets—Sauer, 8 for 133; Snell, 4 for 40; Mathis, 3 for 20; Lammons, 2 for 13.
Baltimore—Richardson, 6 for 58; Orr, 3 for 42; Mackey, 3 for 35; Matte, 2 for 30; Hill, 2 for 1; Mitchell, 1 for 15.

PUNTING
New York Jets—Johnson, 4 for 155, 38.8 average.
Baltimore—Lee, 3 for 144, 44.3 average.

PUNT RETURNS
New York Jets—Baird, 1 for 0, 1 fair catch.
Baltimore—Brown, 4 for 34.

KICKOFF RETURNS
New York Jets—Christy, 1 for 25.
Baltimore—Pearson, 2 for 59; Brown, 2 for 46.

INTERCEPTIONS
New York Jets—Beverly, 2 for 0; Hudson, 1 for 9; Sample, 1 for 0.
Baltimore—None.

Super Bowl IV

Kansas City 23, Minnesota 7

Kansas City—with head coach Hank Stram's crazy-quilt offense—did its homework before Super Bowl IV. The book on Minnesota was that the Vikings liked to score quickly, take control, then tee off on the opposing quarterback with their Purple People Eaters defensive line.

But taking control against the Chiefs would not be easy. In 16 regular-season and playoff games, Kansas City had allowed only seven touchdowns in the first half.

On this day it would allow none, which was remarkable because it was a stormy afternoon and the field was wet. Also remarkable was the fact that quarterback Len Dawson showed up as ready to play as he did. Prior to the game he had to deal with allegations that he had underworld associations.

The story was reported on the Huntley-Brinkley NBC newscast, January 6, 1970. It said a special Justice Department Task Force was about to call seven professional football players to testify about their relationship with known gamblers. Among the players scheduled to testify, it reported, was Dawson (who eventually was cleared on all charges).

Despite this added pressure, Dawson completed his first two passes for 37 yards and Jan Stenerud kicked a 48-yard field goal. He completed three more and Stenerud kicked a 32-yarder.

The Chiefs made the Vikings' heavy rush work against them with Frank Pitts's 19-yard reverse. Then Stenerud came on again and kicked a 25-yarder for a 9-0 lead. The Vikings fumbled the ensuing kickoff, and Dawson supervised a six-play drive, climaxed by Mike Garrett's five-yard touchdown run.

Joe Kapp, Minnesota's charismatic quarterback, rallied for a third-quarter touchdown drive, but the Chiefs countered with one of their own, capped by a 46-yard pass to Otis Taylor.

Defense is what failed Kansas City in Super Bowl I. This time around, it was the key to the Chiefs' success. Minnesota's last three possessions ended with interceptions, and all day was denied a ground game.

And as for Dawson, he was again in the headlines—as Game IV's most valuable player.

Participants—Kansas City Chiefs, champions of the American Football League, and Minnesota Vikings, champions of the National Football League
Date—January 11, 1970
Site—Tulane Stadium, New Orleans
Time—2:35 P.M. CST
Conditions—61, heavy overcast, wet field
Playing Surface—Grass
Television and Radio—Columbia Broadcasting System (CBS)
Regular Season Records—Kansas City, 11-3; Minnesota, 12-2
League Championships—Kansas City defeated the Oakland Raiders 17-7 for the AFL title; Minnesota defeated the Cleveland Browns 27-7 for the NFL title
Players' Shares—$15,000 to each member of the winning team; $7,500 to each member of the losing team
Attendance—80,562
Gross Receipts—$3,817,872.69
Officials—Referee, John McDonough, NFL; umpire, Lou Palazzi, AFL; line judge, Bill Schleibaum, NFL; head linesman, Harry Kessel, NFL; back judge, Tom Kelleher, NFL; field judge, Charley Musser, AFL
Coaches—Hank Stram, Kansas City; Bud Grant, Minnesota

The Chiefs' run defense, including tackle Buck Buchanan (86), held the Vikings to 67 yards.

Minnesota	Starters, Offense	Kansas City
Gene Washington	WR	Frank Pitts
Grady Alderman	LT	Jim Tyrer
Jim Vellone	LG	Ed Budde
Mick Tingelhoff	C	E. J. Holub
Milt Sunde	RG	Mo Moorman
Ron Yary	RT	Dave Hill
John Beasley	TE	Fred Arbanas
John Henderson	WR	Otis Taylor
Joe Kapp	QB	Len Dawson
Dave Osborn	RB	Mike Garrett
Bill Brown	RB	Robert Holmes
	Starters, Defense	
Carl Eller	LE	Jerry Mays
Gary Larsen	LT	Curley Culp
Alan Page	RT	Buck Buchanan
Jim Marshall	RE	Aaron Brown
Roy Winston	LLB	Bobby Bell
Lonnie Warwick	MLB	Willie Lanier
Wally Hilgenberg	RLB	Jim Lynch
Earsell Mackbee	LCB	Jim Marsalis
Ed Sharockman	RCB	Emmitt Thomas
Karl Kassulke	LS	Jim Kearney
Paul Krause	RS	Johnny Robinson

	1	2	3	4		
Minnesota	0	0	7	0	—	7
Kansas City	3	13	7	0	—	23

KC —FG Stenerud 48
KC —FG Stenerud 32
KC —FG Stenerud 25
KC —Garrett 5 run (Stenerud kick)
Minn—Osborn 4 run (Cox kick)
KC —Taylor 46 pass from Dawson (Stenerud kick)

TEAM STATISTICS	Minn	KC
First downs	13	18
Rushing	2	8
Passing	10	7
By penalty	1	3
Total yardage	239	279
Net rushing yardage	67	157
Net passing yardage	172	122
Passes att.-comp.-had int.	28-17-3	17-12-0

RUSHING
Minnesota—Brown, 6 for 26; Reed, 4 for 17; Osborn, 7 for 15, 1 TD; Kapp, 2 for 9.
Kansas City—Garrett, 11 for 39, 1 TD; Pitts, 3 for 37; Hayes, 8 for 31; McVea, 12 for 26; Dawson, 3 for 11; Holmes, 5 for 7.
PASSING
Minnesota—Kapp, 16 of 25 for 183, 2 int.; Cuozzo, 1 of 3 for 16, 1 int.
Kansas City—Dawson, 12 of 17 for 142, 1 TD, 1 int.
RECEIVING
Minnesota—Henderson, 7 for 111; Brown, 3 for 11; Beasley, 2 for 41; Reed, 2 for 16; Osborn, 2 for 11; Washington, 1 for 9.
Kansas City—Taylor, 6 for 81, 1 TD; Pitts, 3 for 33; Garrett, 2 for 25; Hayes, 1 for 3.
PUNTING
Minnesota—Lee, 3 for 111, 37.0 average.
Kansas City—Wilson, 4 for 194, 48.5 average.
PUNT RETURNS
Minnesota—West, 2 for 18.
Kansas City—Garrett, 1 for 0.
KICKOFF RETURNS
Minnesota—West, 3 for 46; Jones, 1 for 33.
Kansas City—Hayes, 2 for 36.
INTERCEPTIONS
Minnesota—Krause, 1 for 0.
Kansas City—Lanier, 1 for 9; Robinson, 1 for 9; Thomas, 1 for 6.

Super Bowl V

Baltimore 16, Dallas 13

This was the first "Super Bowl" (the four previous games had been known as the "AFL-NFL World Championship Game"). All 79,204 seats in the Orange Bowl had been sold and 20,000 more ticket seekers were turned down.

The game was not one for football purists, who counted 16 major mistakes. The Cowboys alone had 10 penalties. There were interceptions, dropped and bad passes, and fumbles.

The day was typified by the first touchdown. Johnny Unitas of the Colts aimed a pass at Eddie Hinton. It caromed off him, ricocheted off Dallas cornerback Mel Renfro, and settled into the hands of Colts tight end John Mackey, who rumbled untouched to complete a record 75-yard play. The extra point was blocked, tying the score 6-6. Later in the quarter, Unitas was injured and Earl Morrall came in.

By the third quarter, the Cowboys led 13-6, but Baltimore pushed to midfield, close enough for Jim O'Brien to try a 52-yard field goal. O'Brien, a rookie, never had kicked a field goal longer than 48 yards, but the Colts were willing to let him try. The kid they called "Lassie" because of his long hair was loose enough to do anything, they figured.

O'Brien's attempt was short, but in keeping with the zaniness of the game, the kick was allowed to roll and died inside the 1-yard line.

Everything seemed to go wrong for the Colts in the second half. They drove to the Dallas 11, but Morrall's pass was intercepted by Chuck Howley in the end zone. They tried a flea-flicker from the Cowboys' 30. It short-circuited; running back Sam Havrilak threw to Hinton, and it might have turned into a touchdown except that Hinton fumbled at the 5 and lost possession.

Still, with a minute to play, Mike Curtis, Baltimore's middle linebacker, intercepted Craig Morton's pass, which had deflected off a leaping Dan Reeves, and returned it 13 yards to Dallas's 28.

With five seconds left, O'Brien lined up to kick a 32-yard field goal. Dallas called time out, but the stalling tactic didn't work. O'Brien's kick sailed true. The Colts were winners and the Super Bowl III loss had been avenged.

Participants—Baltimore Colts, champions of the American Football Conference, and Dallas Cowboys, champions of the National Football Conference
Date—January 17, 1971
Site—Orange Bowl, Miami
Time—2:00 P.M. EST
Conditions—70 degrees, clear skies
Playing Surface—Poly-Turf
Television and Radio—National Broadcasting Company (NBC)
Regular Season Records—Baltimore, 11-2-1; Dallas, 10-4
Conference Championships—Baltimore defeated the Oakland Raiders 27-17 for the AFC title; Dallas defeated the San Francisco 49ers 17-10 for the NFC title
Players' Shares—$15,000 to each member of the winning team; $7,500 to each member of the losing team
Attendance—79,204
Gross Receipts—$3,992,280.01
Officials—Referee, Norm Schachter; umpire, Paul Trepinski; line judge, Jack Fette; head linesman, Ed Marion; back judge, Hugh Gamber; field judge, Fritz Graf
Coaches—Don McCafferty, Baltimore; Tom Landry, Dallas

Linebacker Mike Curtis (32) picked off a deflected pass to set up the Colts' winning field goal.

Baltimore	Starters, Offense	Dallas
Eddie Hinton	WR	Bob Hayes
Bob Vogel	LT	Ralph Neely
Glenn Ressler	LG	John Niland
Bill Curry	C	Dave Manders
John Williams	RG	Blaine Nye
Dan Sullivan	RT	Rayfield Wright
John Mackey	TE	Pettis Norman
Roy Jefferson	WR	Reggie Rucker
Johnny Unitas	QB	Craig Morton
Norm Bulaich	RB	Duane Thomas
Tom Nowatzke	RB	Walt Garrison
Starters, Defense		
Charles (Bubba) Smith	LE	Larry Cole
Billy Ray Smith	LT	Jethro Pugh
Fred Miller	RT	Bob Lilly
Roy Hilton	RE	George Andrie
Ray May	LLB	Dave Edwards
Mike Curtis	MLB	Lee Roy Jordan
Ted Hendricks	RLB	Chuck Howley
Charlie Stukes	LCB	Herb Adderley
Jim Duncan	RCB	Mel Renfro
Jerry Logan	LS	Cornell Green
Rick Volk	RS	Charlie Waters

Baltimore	0	6	0	10	—	16
Dallas	3	10	0	0	—	13

Dall—FG Clark 14
Dall—FG Clark 30
Balt—Mackey 75 pass from Unitas (kick blocked)
Dall—Thomas 7 pass from Morton (Clark kick)
Balt—Nowatzke 2 run (O'Brien kick)
Balt—FG O'Brien 32

TEAM STATISTICS	Balt	Dall
First downs	14	10
Rushing	4	4
Passing	6	5
By penalty	4	1
Total yardage	329	215
Net rushing yardage	69	102
Net passing yardage	260	113
Passes att.-comp.-had int.	25-11-3	26-12-3

RUSHING
Baltimore—Nowatzke, 10 for 33, 1 TD; Bulaich, 18 for 28; Unitas, 1 for 4; Havrilak, 1 for 3; Morrall, 1 for 1.
Dallas—Garrison, 12 for 65; Thomas, 18 for 35; Morton, 1 for 2.
PASSING
Baltimore—Morrall, 7 of 15 for 147, 1 int.; Unitas, 3 of 9 for 88, 1 TD, 2 int.; Havrilak, 1 of 1 for 25.
Dallas—Morton, 12 of 26 for 127, 1 TD, 3 int.
RECEIVING
Baltimore—Jefferson, 3 for 52; Mackey, 2 for 80, 1 TD; Hinton, 2 for 51; Havrilak, 2 for 27; Nowatzke, 1 for 45; Bulaich, 1 for 5.
Dallas—Reeves, 5 for 46; Thomas, 4 for 21, 1 TD; Garrison, 2 for 19; Hayes, 1 for 41.
PUNTING
Baltimore—Lee, 4 for 168, 41.5 average.
Dallas—Widby, 9 for 377, 41.9 average.
PUNT RETURNS
Baltimore—Logan, 1 for 8; Gardin, 4 for 4, 3 fair catches.
Dallas—Hayes, 3 for 9.
KICKOFF RETURNS
Baltimore—Duncan, 4 for 90.
Dallas—Harris, 1 for 18; Hill, 1 for 14; Kiner, 1 for 2.
INTERCEPTIONS
Baltimore—Volk, 1 for 30; Logan, 1 for 14; Curtis, 1 for 13.
Dallas—Howley, 2 for 22; Renfro, 1 for 0.

Super Bowl VI

Dallas 24, Miami 3

The story of Super Bowl VI began at the end of Super Bowl V, with the helmet of Bob Lilly bouncing to midfield after he had slammed it to the turf following the Colts' last-second victory.

Lilly's disgust was a capsule of the Cowboys' past. "Next Year's Champions" they were called, more in jest than prophecy. "They can't win the big one," was their universal indictment.

Not only had the Cowboys lost the last Super Bowl, but they had failed in four divisional or league championship games in the previous four seasons.

Game VI gave them their first retribution—and they've been taking it ever since.

In Dallas's first series of plays on this very cold January day, they ran only once and ended up punting. But by the time the afternoon ended, the Cowboys, with Duane Thomas, Calvin Hill, and Walt Garrison, had run for 252 yards, 92 yards more than Green Bay had piled up in beating Oakland in Super Bowl II.

Dallas ran so successfully because the hub of the Miami defense, middle linebacker Nick Buoniconti, was controlled on virtually every play.

Meanwhile, the vaunted Dolphins' offense was stymied. Larry Csonka, who had not fumbled all season, lost the ball on his second carry of the game. And dangerous Dolphins wide receiver Paul Warfield was shut down by cornerback Mel Renfro and safety Cornell Green.

The Dolphins began wearing down late in the first half. The Cowboys ran seven times on a 76-yard drive and only one rush gained less than five yards. The touchdown came when Roger Staubach, who led Dallas to 10 straight victories after taking over the quarterback job from Craig Morton, passed seven yards to Lance Alworth.

The game was all but over after Dallas took the second-half kickoff. The Cowboys bulled 71 yards for the touchdown, with the enigmatic Thomas accounting for half of them.

"They're too young to win the Super Bowl," said Dallas linebacker Dave Edwards about the Dolphins. However, Miami, which had its first winning season just the year before, would be back.

Participants—Miami Dolphins, champions of the American Football Conference, and Dallas Cowboys, champions of the National Football Conference
Date—January 16, 1972
Site—Tulane Stadium, New Orleans
Time—1:35 P.M. CST
Conditions—39 degrees, sunny
Playing Surface—Poly-Turf
Television and Radio—Columbia Broadcasting System (CBS)
Regular Season Records—Miami, 10-3-1; Dallas, 11-3
Conference Championships—Miami defeated the Baltimore Colts 21-0 for the AFC title; Dallas defeated the San Francisco 49ers 14-3 for the NFC title
Players' Shares—$15,000 to each member of the winning team; $7,500 to each member of the losing team
Attendance—81,023
Gross Receipts—$4,041,527.89
Officials—Referee, Jim Tunney; umpire, Joe Connell; line judge, Art Holst; head linesman, Al Sabato; back judge, Ralph Vandenberg; field judge, Bob Wortman
Coaches—Don Shula, Miami; Tom Landry, Dallas

Dallas ran over Miami in Game VI with Duane Thomas (33) and dominant line blocking.

Dallas	Starters, Offense	Miami
Bob Hayes	WR	Paul Warfield
Tony Liscio	LT	Doug Crusan
John Niland	LG	Bob Kuechenberg
Dave Manders	C	Bob DeMarco
Blaine Nye	RG	Larry Little
Rayfield Wright	RT	Norm Evans
Mike Ditka	TE	Marv Fleming
Lance Alworth	WR	Howard Twilley
Roger Staubach	QB	Bob Griese
Duane Thomas	RB	Jim Kiick
Walt Garrison	RB	Larry Csonka
	Starters, Defense	
Larry Cole	LE	Jim Riley
Jethro Pugh	LT	Manny Fernandez
Bob Lilly	RT	Bob Heinz
George Andrie	RE	Bill Stanfill
Dave Edwards	LLB	Doug Swift
Lee Roy Jordan	MLB	Nick Buoniconti
Chuck Howley	RLB	Mike Kolen
Herb Adderley	LCB	Tim Foley
Mel Renfro	RCB	Curtis Johnson
Cornell Green	LS	Dick Anderson
Cliff Harris	RS	Jake Scott

Dallas	3	7	7	7	—	24
Miami	0	3	0	0	—	3

Dall—FG Clark 9
Dall—Alworth 7 pass from Staubach (Clark kick)
Mia—FG Yepremian 31
Dall—D. Thomas 3 run (Clark kick)
Dall—Ditka 7 pass from Staubach (Clark kick)

TEAM STATISTICS	Dall	Mia
First downs	23	10
Rushing	15	3
Passing	8	7
By penalty	0	0
Total yardage	352	185
Net rushing yardage	252	80
Net passing yardage	100	105
Passes att.-comp.-had int.	19-12-0	23-12-1

RUSHING
Dallas—D. Thomas, 19 for 95, 1 TD; Garrison, 14 for 74; Hill, 7 for 25; Staubach, 5 for 18; Ditka, 1 for 17; Hayes, 1 for 16; Reeves, 1 for 7.
Miami—Csonka, 9 for 40; Kiick, 10 for 40; Griese, 1 for 0.
PASSING
Dallas—Staubach, 12 of 19 for 119, 2 TDs.
Miami—Griese, 12 of 23 for 134, 1 int.
RECEIVING
Dallas—D. Thomas, 3 for 17; Alworth, 2 for 28, 1 TD; Ditka, 2 for 28, 1 TD; Hayes, 2 for 23; Garrison, 2 for 11; Hill, 1 for 12.
Miami—Warfield, 4 for 39; Kiick, 3 for 21; Csonka, 2 for 18; Fleming, 1 for 27; Twilley, 1 for 20; Mandich, 1 for 9.
PUNTING
Dallas—Widby, 5 for 166, 37.2 average.
Miami—Seiple, 5 for 200, 40.0 average.
PUNT RETURNS
Dallas—Hayes, 1 for -1, 1 fair catch; Harris, 2 fair catches.
Miami—Scott, 1 for 21.
KICKOFF RETURNS
Dallas—I. Thomas, 1 for 23; Waters, 1 for 11.
Miami—Morris, 4 for 90; Ginn, 1 for 32.
INTERCEPTIONS
Dallas—Howley, 1 for 41.
Miami—None.

Super Bowl VII
Miami 14, Washington 7

It was the No Names versus the Over-the-Hill Gang, a western-style gunfight in the Los Angeles Memorial Coliseum with 90,182 in the stands and 75 million watching on television.

Washington got its nickname the season before, when George Allen became the head coach and traded for veteran talent others felt was "over the hill."

It was Tom Landry's unwitting comment before Super Bowl VI that gave Miami's defense its name: "I can't recall their names, but they are a matter of great concern to us."

History weighed heavily on the Dolphins. They were unbeaten in 16 games. No previous NFL team ever played an entire season without losing. The cynics doubted that Miami could keep the streak alive. That doubt began to erode in the first quarter when Bob Griese, out most of the season with a broken ankle, completed a 28-yard pass for a touchdown to Howard Twilley. Twilley carried defender Pat Fischer five yards into the end zone. (Griese passed only 11 times all day, completing 8.)

Another Miami touchdown was nullified by a penalty, but middle linebacker Nick Buoniconti intercepted a pass and returned it 32 yards to the Redskins' 27. Jim Kiick eventually plunged a yard for the second touchdown.

The No-Names made big play after big play to frustrate Washington. Safety Jake Scott stopped two Redskins drives with interceptions, and the line shut down Larry Brown, the NFC's loading rusher. It wasn't until the final two minutes that the Redskins scored on the game's most memorable—and most unusual—play. Bill Brundige blocked a field goal. Miami kicker Garo Yepremian picked it up and fumbled attempting to pass. Mike Bass of the Redskins recovered and ran 49 yards to score.

"This team has gone into an area that no other team has gone before," said Dolphins coach Don Shula, for whom the victory was personal redemption after two previous Super Bowl losses (one with Baltimore).

"In the past, there was always the feeling of not having achieved the ultimate. This is the ultimate."

Participants—Miami Dolphins, champions of the American Football Conference, and Washington Redskins, champions of the National Football Conference
Date—January 14, 1973
Site—Los Angeles Memorial Coliseum
Time—12:30 P.M. PST
Conditions—84 degrees, sunny, hazy
Playing Surface—Grass
Television and Radio—National Broadcasting Company (NBC)
Regular Season Records—Miami, 14-0; Washington, 11-3
Conference Championships—Miami defeated the Pittsburgh Steelers 21-17 for the AFC title; Washington defeated the Dallas Cowboys 26-3 for the NFC title
Players' Shares—$15,000 to each member of the winning team; $7,500 to each member of the losing team
Attendance—90,182
Gross Receipts—$4,180,086.53
Officials—Referee, Tommy Bell; umpire, Lou Palazzi; line judge, Bruce Alford; head linesman, Tony Veteri; back judge, Tom Kelleher; field judge, Tony Skover
Coaches—Don Shula, Miami; George Allen, Washington

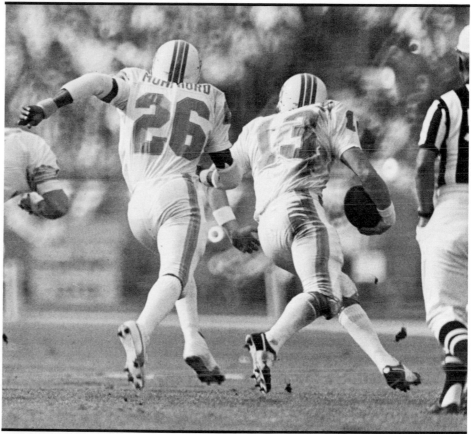

Jake Scott's (13) two interception returns for 63 yards helped keep Miami's record perfect.

Miami	Starters, Offense	Washington
Paul Warfield	WR	Charley Taylor
Wayne Moore	LT	Terry Hermeling
Bob Kuechenberg	LG	Paul Laaveg
Jim Langer	C	Len Hauss
Larry Little	RG	John Wilbur
Norm Evans	RT	Walter Rock
Marv Fleming	TE	Jerry Smith
Howard Twilley	WR	Roy Jefferson
Bob Greise	QB	Billy Kilmer
Jim Kiick	RB	Larry Brown
Larry Csonka	RB	Charley Harraway
	Starters, Defense	
Vern Den Herder	LE	Ron McDole
Manny Fernandez	LT	Bill Brundige
Bob Heinz	RT	Diron Talbert
Bill Stanfill	RE	Verlon Biggs
Doug Swift	LLB	Jack Pardee
Nick Buoniconti	MLB	Myron Pottios
Mike Kolen	RLB	Chris Hanburger
Lloyd Mumphord	LCB	Pat Fischer
Curtis Johnson	RCB	Mike Bass
Dick Anderson	LS	Brig Owens
Jake Scott	RS	Roosevelt Taylor

Miami	7	7	0	0	—	14
Washington	0	0	0	7	—	7

Mia —Twilley 28 pass from Griese (Yepremian kick)
Mia —Kiick 1 run (Yepremian kick)
Wash—Bass 49 fumble recovery return (Knight kick)

TEAM STATISTICS	Mia	Wash
First downs	12	16
Rushing	7	9
Passing	5	7
By penalty	0	0
Total yardage	253	228
Net rushing yardage	184	141
Net passing yardage	69	87
Passes att.-comp.-had int.	11-8-1	28-14-3

RUSHING
Miami—Csonka, 15 for 112; Kiick, 12 for 38, 1 TD; Morris, 10 for 34.
Washington—Brown, 22 for 72; Harraway, 10 for 37; Kilmer, 2 for 18; C. Taylor, 1 for 8; Smith, 1 for 6.
PASSING
Miami—Griese, 8 of 11 for 88, 1 TD, 1 int.
Washington—Kilmer, 14 of 28 for 104, 3 int.
RECEIVING
Miami—Warfield, 3 for 36; Kiick, 2 for 6; Twilley, 1 for 28, 1 TD; Mandich, 1 for 19; Csonka, 1 for -1.
Washington—Jefferson, 5 for 50; Brown, 5 for 26; C. Taylor, 2 for 20; Smith, 1 for 11; Harraway, 1 for -3.
PUNTING
Miami—Seiple, 7 for 301, 43.0 average.
Washington—Bragg, 5 for 156, 31.2 average.
PUNT RETURNS
Miami—Scott, 2 for 4, 2 fair catches; Anderson, 2 fair catches.
Washington—Haymond, 4 for 9; Vactor, 2 fair catches.
KICKOFF RETURNS
Miami—Morris, 2 for 33.
Washington—Haymond, 2 for 30; Mul-Key, 1 for 15.
INTERCEPTIONS
Miami—Scott, 2 for 63; Buoniconti, 1 for 32.
Washington—Owens, 1 for 0.

Super Bowl VIII
Miami 24, Minnesota 7

It is the third quarter. The score is Miami 17, Minnesota 0. The Dolphins have the ball on the Vikings' 2-yard line. Suddenly, Bob Griese, about to take the snap from center, whirls and asks: "What the hell is the snap count?"

"One," says running back Jim Kiick.

"Two," says fullback Larry Csonka.

Griese takes Csonka's word. It is an error. When Griese gets the ball, Kiick and Csonka are still in their three-point stances. Nevertheless, Csonka roars ahead, takes the handoff, and plunges into the end zone.

Super Bowl VIII was virtually over before it began. Minnesota had won 14 games, but the Vikings were ranked twenty-third among the 26 NFL teams in stopping the run. Miami, which had emerged as one of the most relentless running teams of all time, took advantage of Minnesota's weakness with well-conceived misdirection plays. It also threw its "53" defense, one of the earliest of the 3-4s, at the Vikings.

Griese, who threw only 11 passes in the previous Super Bowl, passed only seven times this day, completing six.

But the game belonged more to players such as Csonka, a massive rusher; Jim Langer, a pit bull of a center; and Bob Kuechenberg, a tenacious guard. Csonka gained a record 145 yards on 33 carries and scored two touchdowns.

But his path was cleared, sometimes yards beyond the line of scrimmage, by Langer and Kuechenberg, who took turns controlling Alan Page, the quick Vikings defensive tackle.

Page was asked when Miami began to look invincible. "After the first couple of plays," he admitted.

Csonka, an old-fashioned type of player, gave his blockers full credit. "I never got touched until I got to the secondary," he said.

"They just did everything to us on the running game," said Vikings defensive end Carl Eller. "Sweeps, traps, whatever."

There was a certain sadness, though, pervading the Dolphins' victory. There was a feeling, which proved accurate, that this was a last hurrah for the team, that it would be breaking up.

"The only adjective that fits this team is 'great,'" said jubilant coach Don Shula.

Participants—Miami Dolphins, champions of the American Football Conference, and Minnesota Vikings, champions of the National Football Conference
Date—January 13, 1974
Site—Rice Stadium, Houston
Time—2:30 P.M. CST
Conditions—50 degrees, overcast
Playing Surface—AstroTurf
Television and Radio—Columbia Broadcasting System (CBS)
Regular Season Records—Miami, 12-2; Minnesota, 12-2
Conference Championships—Miami defeated the Oakland Raiders 27-10 for the AFC title; Minnesota defeated the Dallas Cowboys 27-10 for the NFC title
Players' Shares—$15,000 to each member of the winning team; $7,500 to each member of the losing team
Attendance—68,142
Gross Receipts—$3,953,641.22
Officials—Referee, Ben Dreith; umpire, Ralph Morcroft; line judge, Jack Fette; head linesman, Leo Miles; back judge, Stan Javie; field judge, Fritz Graf
Coaches—Don Shula, Miami; Bud Grant, Minnesota

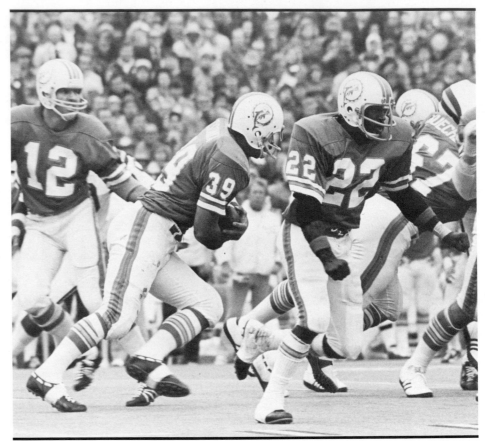

Miami's Larry Csonka (39) blasted for 145 yards and two touchdowns in Super Bowl VIII.

Minnesota	Starters, Offense	Miami
Carroll Dale	WR	Paul Warfield
Grady Alderman	LT	Wayne Moore
Ed White	LG	Bob Kuechenberg
Mick Tingelhoff	C	Jim Langer
Frank Gallagher	RG	Larry Little
Ron Yary	RT	Norm Evans
Stu Voigt	TE	Jim Mandich
John Gilliam	WR	Marlin Briscoe
Fran Tarkenton	QB	Bob Griese
Chuck Foreman	RB	Eugene (Mercury) Morris
Oscar Reed	RB	Larry Csonka
	Starters, Defense	
Carl Eller	LE	Vern Den Herder
Gary Larsen	LT	Manny Fernandez
Alan Page	RT	Bob Heinz
Jim Marshall	RE	Bill Stanfill
Roy Winston	LLB	Doug Swift
Jeff Siemon	MLB	Nick Buoniconti
Wally Hilgenberg	RLB	Mike Kolen
Nate Wright	LCB	Lloyd Mumphord
Bobby Bryant	RCB	Curtis Johnson
Jeff Wright	LS	Dick Anderson
Paul Krause	RS	Jake Scott

Minnesota	0	0	0	7	—	7
Miami	14	3	7	0	—	24

Mia —Csonka 5 run (Yepremian kick)
Mia —Kiick 1 run (Yepremian kick)
Mia —FG Yepremian 28
Mia —Csonka 2 run (Yepremian kick)
Minn—Tarkenton 4 run (Cox kick)

TEAM STATISTICS	Minn	Mia
First downs	14	21
Rushing	5	13
Passing	8	4
By penalty	1	4
Total yardage	238	259
Net rushing yardage	72	196
Net passing yardage	166	63
Passes att.-comp.-had int.	28-18-1	7-6-0

RUSHING
Minnesota—Reed, 11 for 32; Foreman, 7 for 18; Tarkenton, 4 for 17, 1 TD; Marinaro, 1 for 3; B. Brown, 1 for 2.
Miami—Csonka, 33 for 145, 2 TDs; Morris, 11 for 34; Kiick, 7 for 10, 1 TD; Griese, 2 for 7.
PASSING
Minnesota—Tarkenton, 18 of 28 for 182, 1 int.
Miami—Griese, 6 of 7 for 73.
RECEIVING
Minnesota—Foreman, 5 for 27; Gilliam, 4 for 44; Voigt, 3 for 46; Marinaro, 2 for 39; B. Brown, 1 for 9; Kingsriter, 1 for 9; Lash, 1 for 9; Reed, 1 for -1.
Miami—Warfield, 2 for 33; Mandich, 2 for 21; Briscoe, 2 for 19.
PUNTING
Minnesota—Eischeid, 5 for 211, 42.2 average.
Miami—Seiple, 3 for 119, 39.7 average.
PUNT RETURNS
Minnesota—Bryant, 1 fair catch.
Miami—Scott, 3 for 20, 1 fair catch.
KICKOFF RETURNS
Minnesota—Gilliam, 2 for 41; West, 2 for 28.
Miami—Scott, 2 for 47.
INTERCEPTIONS
Minnesota—None.
Miami—Johnson, 1 for 10.

Super Bowl IX
Pittsburgh 16, Minnesota 6

It had taken the Pittsburgh Steelers 42 years to get to the championship game of the NFL and now it looked as if they were sleep-walking through it. They led at halftime, but the score was a mere 2-0 against a Minnesota team that could generate almost no offense.

Something happened, though, in the last two minutes of the second quarter that seemed to jar the Steelers awake.

Vikings receiver John Gilliam cut across the middle, deep in Pittsburgh territory. Fran Tarkenton hit him on the numbers, but Steelers safety Glen Edwards hit him even harder. Gilliam fumbled and Mel Blount recovered for Pittsburgh.

Instead of having a first down on the Steelers' 5, the Vikings had seen their best scoring chance dissipate. In fact, their only score would come in the fourth quarter on a blocked punt recovered for a touchdown.

The Pittsburgh defense, called the Steel Curtain, had been built painstakingly by Chuck Noll, who became head coach of the team in 1969.

After winning their first game under Noll, the Steelers lost their next 13. The fans were clamoring for offensive stars, but in his first draft Noll took Joe Greene, a defensive tackle from North Texas State. A Pittsburgh newspaper asked "Joe Who?" in its headline.

In time they found out about Greene, and also about Blount, L.C. Greenwood, Jack Ham, Jack Lambert, Andy Russell, and Dwight White, the steel of the Steel Curtain.

Noll's hand-picked defense arrived earlier than the offense. In that first championship season the quarterback job floated among Terry Bradshaw, Joe Gilliam, and Terry Hanratty. Bradshaw finally got it back late in the year. Franco Harris, the main ball carrier, gained only 125 yards in his first three games, then gained 881 in his last nine, when he was fully healthy.

By the end of Game IX, Harris had a Super Bowl record 158 yards and a 12-yard touchdown run.

But it was the Steelers' defense that reigned, allowing the Vikings just 17 rushing yards and only 102 yards passing.

Participants—Pittsburgh Steelers, champions of the American Football Conference, and Minnesota Vikings, champions of the National Football Conference
Date—January 12, 1975
Site—Tulane Stadium, New Orleans
Time—2:00 P.M. CST
Conditions—46 degrees, cloudy
Playing Surface—Poly-Turf
Television and Radio—National Broadcasting Company (NBC)
Regular Season Records—Pittsburgh, 10-3-1; Minnesota, 10-4
Conference Championships—Pittsburgh defeated the Oakland Raiders 24-13 for the AFC title; Minnesota defeated the Los Angeles Rams 14-10 for the NFC title
Players' Shares—$15,000 to each member of the winning team; $7,500 to each member of the losing team
Attendance—80,997
Gross Receipts—$5,259,766.90
Officials—Referee, Bernie Ulman; umpire, Al Conway; line judge, Bruce Alford; head linesman, Ed Marion; back judge, Ray Douglas; field judge, Dick Dolack
Coaches—Chuck Noll, Pittsburgh; Bud Grant, Minnesota

Owner Art Rooney's patience was rewarded with the Steelers' first Super Bowl trophy.

Pittsburgh	Starters, Offense	Minnesota
Frank Lewis	WR	Jim Lash
Jon Kolb	LT	Charles Goodrum
Jim Clack	LG	Andy Maurer
Ray Mansfield	C	Mick Tingelhoff
Gerry Mullins	RG	Ed White
Gordon Gravelle	RT	Ron Yary
Larry Brown	TE	Stu Voigt
Ron Shanklin	WR	John Gilliam
Terry Bradshaw	QB	Fran Tarkenton
Rocky Bleier	RB	Chuck Foreman
Franco Harris	RB	Dave Osborn
	Starters, Defense	
L. C. Greenwood	LE	Carl Eller
Joe Greene	LT	Doug Sutherland
Ernie Holmes	RT	Alan Page
Dwight White	RE	Jim Marshall
Jack Ham	LLB	Roy Winston
Jack Lambert	MLB	Jeff Siemon
Andy Russell	RLB	Wally Hilgenberg
J. T. Thomas	LCB	Nate Wright
Mel Blount	RCB	Jackie Wallace
Mike Wagner	LS	Jeff Wright
Glen Edwards	RS	Paul Krause

Pittsburgh	0	2	7	7	16
Minnesota	0	0	0	6	6

Pitt —Safety, White downed Tarkenton in end zone
Pitt — Harris 12 run (Gerela kick)
Minn—T. Brown recovered blocked punt in end zone (kick failed)
Pitt —L. Brown 4 pass from Bradshaw (Gerela kick)

TEAM STATISTICS	Pitt	Minn
First downs	17	9
Rushing	11	2
Passing	5	5
By penalty	1	2
Total yardage	333	119
Net rushing yardage	249	17
Net passing yardage	84	102
Passes att.-comp.-had int.	14-9-0	26-11-3

RUSHING
Pittsburgh—Harris, 34 for 158, 1 TD; Bleier, 17 for 65; Bradshaw, 5 for 33; Swann, 1 for -7.
Minnesota—Foreman, 12 for 18; Tarkenton, 1 for 0; Osborn, 8 for -1.
PASSING
Pittsburgh—Bradshaw, 9 of 14 for 97, 1 TD.
Minnesota—Tarkenton, 11 of 26 for 102, 3 int.
RECEIVING
Pittsburgh—Brown, 3 for 49, 1 TD; Stallworth, 3 for 24; Bleier, 2 for 11; Lewis, 1 for 12.
Minnesota—Foreman, 5 for 50; Voigt, 2 for 31; Osborn, 2 for 7; Gilliam, 1 for 16; Reed, 1 for -2.
PUNTING
Pittsburgh—Walden, 7 for 243, 34.7 average.
Minnesota—Eischeid, 6 for 223, 37.2 average.
PUNT RETURNS
Pittsburgh—Swann, 3 for 34; Edwards, 2 for 2.
Minnesota—McCullum, 3 for 11; N. Wright, 1 for 1; Wallace, 1 fair catch.
KICKOFF RETURNS
Pittsburgh—Harrison, 2 for 17; Pearson, 1 for 15.
Minnesota—McCullum, 1 for 26; McClanahan, 1 for 22; B. Brown, 1 for 2.
INTERCEPTIONS
Pittsburgh—Wagner, 1 for 26; Blount, 1 for 10; Greene, 1 for 10.
Minnesota—None.

Super Bowl X

Pittsburgh 21, Dallas 17

This was the Bicentennial Super Bowl. It also was the Hollywood Super Bowl; scenes for the film *Black Sunday* were being shot during the game, which had enough action, excitement, and drama to be a feature film itself.

Dallas, the first wild card team ever to reach the Super Bowl, scored first when the Steelers' punter Bobby Walden took his eyes off the snap and the ball got away from him. Billy Joe DuPree tackled him on the Pittsburgh 29. On the next play, Roger Staubach, playing with injured ribs, passed down the middle to Drew Pearson, who split the defense at the 14 and raced into the end zone.

It was the first time all season the Steelers had yielded a point in the first quarter. Pittsburgh stormed back. Terry Bradshaw passed 32 yards to Lynn Swann, who made a leaping catch at the sideline, then 7 yards to tight end Randy Grossman for a touchdown. Swann had made only a cameo appearance in the previous Super Bowl and for a while it seemed he wouldn't play at all in this one. He had been knocked out of the AFC Championship Game by Oakland and spent the next three days in a hospital recovering from a concussion.

The Steelers' defense was savage, sacking Roger Staubach seven times, three each by L.C. Greenwood and Dwight White, and intercepting him three times.

The defensive pressure—and Jack Lambert's fierce play—produced eight unanswered points (two field goals and a safety), which gave Pittsburgh a 15-10 lead. Then, late in the fourth quarter, Bradshaw went for the jugular. It was third and four from the Pittsburgh 36. Dallas blitzed.

Linebacker D.D. Lewis was just a trifle off course. Cliff Harris arrived a split second too late from his safety spot. Bradshaw's pass went far downfield to Swann, covered by just one man, Mark Washington.

Washington tried valiantly, but Swann made another spectacular, leaping reception and the Steelers had a 64-yard touchdown.

Staubach came up with some last-second heroics of his own, but Dallas fell short. The Steelers prevailed 21-17.

Participants—Pittsburgh Steelers, champions of the American Football Conference, and Dallas Cowboys, champions of the National Football Conference
Date—January 18, 1976
Site—Orange Bowl, Miami
Time—2:00 P.M. EST
Conditions—57 degrees, clear
Playing Surface—Poly-Turf
Television and Radio—Columbia Broadcasting System (CBS)
Regular Season Records—Pittsburgh, 12-2; Dallas, 10-4
Conference Championships—Pittsburgh defeated the Oakland Raiders 16-10 for the AFC title; Dallas defeated the Los Angeles Rams 37-7 for the NFC title
Players' Shares—$15,000 to each member of the winning team; $7,500 to each member of the losing team
Attendance—80,187
Gross Receipts—$5,242,641.25
Officials—Referee, Norm Schachter; umpire, Joe Connell; line judge, Jack Fette; head linesman, Leo Miles; back judge, Stan Javie; field judge, Bill O'Brien
Coaches—Chuck Noll, Pittsburgh; Tom Landry, Dallas

Linebacker Jack Lambert (58) brought the Steel Curtain crashing down on the Cowboys.

Dallas	Starters, Offense	Pittsburgh
Golden Richards	WR	John Stallworth
Ralph Neely	LT	Jon Kolb
Burton Lawless	LG	Jim Clack
John Fitzgerald	C	Ray Mansfield
Blaine Nye	RG	Gerry Mullins
Rayfield Wright	RT	Gordon Gravelle
Jean Fugett	TE	Larry Brown
Drew Pearson	WR	Lynn Swann
Roger Staubach	QB	Terry Bradshaw
Preston Pearson	RB	Rocky Bleier
Robert Newhouse	RB	Franco Harris
	Starters, Defense	
Ed Jones	LE	L. C. Greenwood
Jethro Pugh	LT	Joe Greene
Larry Cole	RT	Ernie Holmes
Harvey Martin	RE	Dwight White
Dave Edwards	LLB	Jack Ham
Lee Roy Jordan	MLB	Jack Lambert
D. D. Lewis	RLB	Andy Russell
Mark Washington	LCB	J. T. Thomas
Mel Renfro	RCB	Mel Blount
Charlie Waters	LS	Mike Wagner
Cliff Harris	RS	Glen Edwards

Dallas	7	3	0	7	—	17
Pittsburgh	7	0	0	14	—	21

Dall—D. Pearson 29 pass from Staubach (Fritsch kick)
Pitt —Grossman 7 pass from Bradshaw (Gerela kick)
Dall—FG Fritsch 36
Pitt —Safety, Harrison blocked Hoopes' punt through end zone
Pitt —FG Gerela 36
Pitt —FG Gerela 18
Pitt —Swann 64 pass from Bradshaw (kick failed)
Dall—P. Howard 34 pass from Staubach (Fritsch kick)

TEAM STATISTICS	Dall	Pitt
First downs	14	13
Rushing	6	7
Passing	8	6
By penalty	0	0
Total yardage	270	339
Net rushing yardage	108	149
Net passing yardage	162	190
Passes att.-comp.-had int.	24-15-3	19-9-0

RUSHING
Dallas—Newhouse, 16 for 56; Staubach, 5 for 22; Dennison, 5 for 16; P. Pearson, 5 for 14.
Pittsburgh—Harris, 27 for 82; Bleier, 15 for 51; Bradshaw, 4 for 16.

PASSING
Dallas—Staubach, 15 of 24 for 204, 2 TDs, 3 int.
Pittsburgh—Bradshaw, 9 of 19 for 209, 2 TDs.

RECEIVING
Dallas—P. Pearson, 5 for 53; Young, 3 for 31; D. Pearson, 2 for 59, 1 TD; Newhouse, 2 for 12; P. Howard, 1 for 34, 1 TD; Fugett, 1 for 9; Dennison, 1 for 6.
Pittsburgh—Swann, 4 for 161, 1 TD; Stallworth, 2 for 8; Harris, 1 for 26; Grossman, 1 for 7; L. Brown, 1 for 7.

PUNTING
Dallas—Hoopes, 7 for 245, 35.0 average.
Pittsburgh—Walden, 4 for 159, 39.8 average.

PUNT RETURNS
Dallas—Richards, 1 for 5, 3 fair catches.
Pittsburgh—D. Brown, 3 for 14; Edwards, 2 for 17.

KICKOFF RETURNS
Dallas—T. Henderson, 48 after a lateral; P. Pearson, 4 for 48.
Pittsburgh—Blount, 3 for 64; Collier, 1 for 25.

INTERCEPTIONS
Dallas—None.
Pittsburgh—Edwards, 1 for 35; Thomas, 1 for 35; Wagner, 1 for 19.

Super Bowl XI

Oakland 32, Minnesota 14

Three times the Minnesota Vikings had gone to a Super Bowl and each time they had been defeated.

This time, against Oakland, they swore it would be different. "This team has a new dimension," said coach Bud Grant. "Emotion."

Grant seemed like a prophet when, late in the opening quarter, Minnesota did what no other team had done before—blocked one of Ray Guy's punts. Fred McNeill, who had knifed in to make the block, recovered on the Oakland 3.

The Vikings desperately needed a touchdown. Not only would it put them ahead for the first time in a Super Bowl game, it would give them precious momentum. But on their second play, they fumbled. Linebacker Phil Villapiano smashed into running back Brent McClanahan, and Willie Hall recovered for the Raiders.

Oakland then drove 90 yards, and Errol Mann kicked a 24-yard field goal.

The matchup between Jim Marshall and Art Shell became a microcosm of the game itself; Marshall, the savvy, determined, 240-pound Vikings defensive end, versus Shell, the savvy, massive 285-pound Raiders offensive tackle. Shell, and with him the Raiders, won.

With Ken Stabler passing to Fred Biletnikoff and Dave Casper, with Oakland's runners churning behind Shell and guard Gene Upshaw, Oakland rolled up a 19-0 lead before Minnesota scored.

"We have a bunch of renegades who play well together," explained Stabler.

Four of those renegades, Upshaw, Biletnikoff, Pete Banaszak, and Willie Brown, had played on the Oakland team beaten by Green Bay in Super Bowl II.

Their moment of fulfillment was assured when Brown streaked 75 yards with a fourth-quarter interception for a touchdown and a 32-7 lead.

The Raiders, who gained a record-breaking 429 yards, won their first National Football League title before a record Super Bowl crowd (103,438) plus 81 million television viewers, the largest audience ever to watch a sporting event.

Participants—Oakland Raiders, champions of the American Football Conference, and Minnesota Vikings, champions of the National Football Conference
Date—January 9, 1977
Site—Rose Bowl, Pasadena
Time—12:30 P.M. PST
Conditions—58 degrees, clear and sunny
Playing Surface—Grass
Television and Radio—National Broadcasting Company (NBC)
Regular Season Records—Oakland, 13-1; Minnesota, 11-2-1
Conference Championships—Oakland defeated the Pittsburgh Steelers 24-7 for the AFC title; Minnesota defeated the Los Angeles Rams 24-13 for the NFC title
Players' Shares—$15,000 to each member of the winning team; $7,500 to each member of the losing team
Attendance—103,438
Gross Receipts—$5,768,772.73
Officials—Referee, Jim Tunney; umpire, Lou Palazzi; line judge, Bill Swanson; head linesman, Ed Marion; back judge, Tom Kelleher; field judge, Armen Terzian
Coaches—John Madden, Oakland; Bud Grant, Minnesota

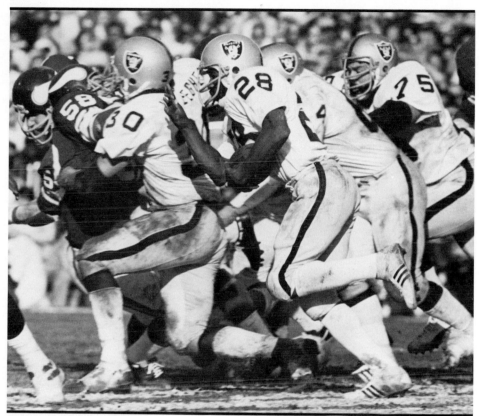

Oakland turned back Minnesota's fourth Super Bowl victory bid with a punishing ground game.

Oakland	Starters, Offense	Minnesota
Clifford Branch	WR	Ahmad Rashad
Art Shell	LT	Steve Riley
Gene Upshaw	LG	Charles Goodrum
Dave Dalby	C	Mick Tingelhoff
George Buehler	RG	Ed White
John Vella	RT	Ron Yary
Dave Casper	TE	Stu Voigt
Fred Biletnikoff	WR	Sammy White
Ken Stabler	QB	Fran Tarkenton
Mark van Eeghen	RB	Chuck Foreman
Clarence Davis	RB	Brent McClanahan
	Starters, Defense	
John Matuszak	LE	Carl Eller
Dave Rowe	NT-LT	Doug Sutherland
Otis Sistrunk	RE-RT	Alan Page
Phil Villapiano	LOLB-RE	Jim Marshall
Monte Johnson	LILB-LLB	Matt Blair
Willie Hall	RILB-MLB	Jeff Siemon
Ted Hendricks	ROLB-RLB	Wally Hilgenberg
Alonzo (Skip) Thomas	LCB	Nate Wright
Willie Brown	RCB	Bobby Bryant
George Atkinson	LS	Jeff Wright
Jack Tatum	RS	Paul Krause

Oakland	0	16	3	13	—	32
Minnesota	0	0	7	7	—	14

Oak—FG Mann 24
Oak—Casper 1 pass from Stabler (Mann kick)
Oak—Banaszak 1 run (kick failed)
Oak—FG Mann 40
Minn—S. White 8 pass from Tarkenton (Cox kick)
Oak—Banaszak 2 run (Mann kick)
Oak—Brown 75 interception return (kick failed)
Minn—Voigt 13 pass from Lee (Cox kick)

TEAM STATISTICS	Oak	Minn
First downs	21	20
Rushing	13	2
Passing	8	15
By penalty	0	3
Total yardage	429	353
Net rushing yardage	266	71
Net passing yardage	163	282
Passes att.-comp.-had int.	19-12-0	44-24-2

RUSHING
Oakland—Davis, 16 for 137; van Eeghen, 18 for 73; Garrett, 4 for 19; Banaszak, 10 for 19, 2 TDs; Ginn, 2 for 9; Rae, 2 for 9.
Minnesota—Foreman, 17 for 44; Johnson, 2 for 9; S. White, 1 for 7; Lee, 1 for 4; Miller, 2 for 4; McClanahan, 3 for 3.
PASSING
Oakland—Stabler, 12 of 19 for 180, 1 TD.
Minnesota—Tarkenton, 17 of 35 for 205, 1 TD, 2 int.; Lee, 7 of 9 for 81, 1 TD.
RECEIVING
Oakland—Biletnikoff, 4 for 79; Casper, 4 for 70, 1 TD; Branch, 3 for 20; Garrett, 1 for 11.
Minnesota—S. White, 5 for 77, 1 TD; Foreman, 5 for 62; Voigt, 4 for 49, 1 TD; Miller, 4 for 19; Rashad, 3 for 53; Johnson, 3 for 26.
PUNTING
Oakland—Guy, 4 for 162, 40.5 average.
Minnesota—Clabo, 7 for 265, 37.9 average.
PUNT RETURNS
Oakland—Colzie, 4 for 43.
Minnesota—Willis, 3 for 57.
KICKOFF RETURNS
Oakland—Garrett, 2 for 47; Siani, 1 for 0.
Minnesota—S. White, 4 for 79; Willis, 3 for 57.
INTERCEPTIONS
Oakland—Brown, 1 for 75, 1 TD; Hall, 1 for 16.
Minnesota—None.

Super Bowl XII

Dallas 27, Denver 10

Dallas's opening play was a fumble, but it also was a message. Tom Landry's call was for a double reverse. Butch Johnson fumbled the last exchange of the ball, but recovered for a nine-yard loss.

"Landry was warning them [the Denver Broncos] to look for anything," said Cliff Harris, the Cowboys' safety. "Landry was letting them know they had to stay at home."

Immobilizing the Denver defense, the intense play of which had made the Broncos the surprise team of the season, was sound practice. The Broncos would manage to sack Roger Staubach five times. They would force six fumbles.

But Denver still had to worry about Dallas's unpredictability. It was such that Landry was ready to use a special play in which Staubach was to end up the receiver, but it was never needed.

Nevertheless, this was to be a defensive game, a clash of nicknamed units—Denver's Orange Crush against Dallas's Doomsday II—that was dominated by the Cowboys.

That was evident in Denver's first three possessions: Craig Morton was sacked by Randy White for an 11-yard loss to end the first; Randy Hughes intercepted Morton to end the second; and Aaron Kyle intercepted Morton to finish the third.

Denver had the ball eight times in the first half and turned it over six times, either by interception or fumble. Yet the Cowboys' lead was just 13-0.

It took one of the great catches in Super Bowl history, Johnson's reception of Staubach's 45-yard pass in the end zone, to break open the game in the third quarter.

The finishing touch came midway through the fourth quarter when fullback Robert Newhouse pulled up short in the midst of a sweep to the left and fired a 29-yard pass to Golden Richards for a touchdown.

Just how much the Dallas defense controlled the game was recognized when White and Harvey Martin were named co-winners of the most valuable player award. Martin put the honor in perspective when he said: "We feel we are representing our entire line."

Participants—Denver Broncos, champions of the American Football Conference, and Dallas Cowboys, champions of the National Football Conference
Date—January 15, 1978
Site—Louisiana Superdome, New Orleans
Time—5:15 P.M. CST
Conditions—70 degrees, indoors
Playing Surface—AstroTurf
Television and Radio—Columbia Broadcasting System (CBS)
Regular Season Records—Denver, 12-2; Dallas, 12-2
Conference Championships—Denver defeated the Oakland Raiders 20-17 for the AFC title; Dallas defeated the Minnesota Vikings 23-6 for the NFC title
Players' Shares—$18,000 to each member of the winning team; $9,000 to each member of the losing team
Attendance—75,583
Gross Receipts—$6,923,141.50
Officials—Referee, Jim Tunney; umpire, Joe Connell; line judge, Art Holst; head linesman, Tony Veteri; back judge, Ray Douglas; field judge, Bob Wortman
Coaches—Red Miller, Denver; Tom Landry, Dallas

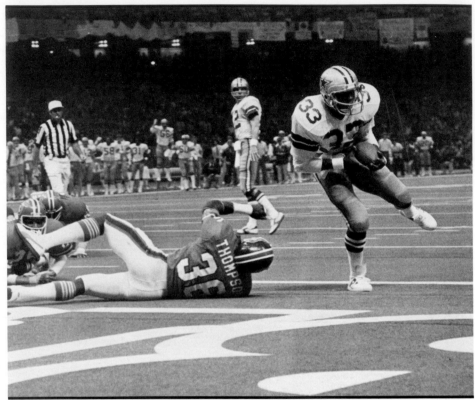

Tony Dorsett (33) put the Cowboys ahead early; the Doomsday II defense took it from there.

Dallas	Starters, Offense	Denver
Butch Johnson	WR	Jack Dolbin
Ralph Neely	LT	Andy Maurer
Herbert Scott	LG	Tom Glassic
John Fitzgerald	C	Mike Montler
Tom Rafferty	RG	Paul Howard
Pat Donovan	RT	Claudie Minor
Billy Joe DuPree	TE	Riley Odoms
Drew Pearson	WR	Haven Moses
Roger Staubach	QB	Craig Morton
Robert Newhouse	RB	Jon Keyworth
Tony Dorsett	RB	Otis Armstrong
	Starters, Defense	
Ed Jones	LE	Barney Chavous
Jethro Pugh	LT-NT	Rubin Carter
Randy White	RT-RE	Lyle Alzado
Harvey Martin	RE-LOLB	Bob Swenson
Thomas Henderson	LLB-LILB	Joe Rizzo
Bob Breunig	MLB-RILB	Randy Gradishar
D. D. Lewis	RLB-ROLB	Tom Jackson
Benny Barnes	LCB	Louis Wright
Aaron Kyle	RCB	Steve Foley
Charlie Waters	LS	Billy Thompson
Cliff Harris	RS	Bernard Jackson

Dallas	10	3	7	7	—	27
Denver	0	0	10	0	—	10

Dall—Dorsett 3 run (Herrera kick)
Dall—FG Herrera 35
Dall—FG Herrera 43
Den—FG Turner 47
Dall—Johnson 45 pass from Staubach (Herrera kick)
Den—Lytle 1 run (Turner kick)
Dall—Richards 29 pass from Newhouse (Herrera kick)

TEAM STATISTICS	Dall	Den
First downs	17	11
Rushing	8	8
Passing	8	1
By penalty	1	2
Total yardage	325	156
Net rushing yardage	143	121
Net passing yardage	182	35
Passes att.-comp.-had int.	28-19-0	25-8-4

RUSHING
Dallas—Dorsett, 15 for 66, 1 TD; Newhouse, 14 for 55; D. White, 1 for 13; P. Pearson, 3 for 11; Staubach, 3 for 6; Laidlaw, 1 for 1; Johnson, 1 for -9.
Denver—Lytle, 10 for 35, 1 TD; Armstrong, 7 for 27; Weese, 3 for 26; Jensen, 1 for 16; Keyworth, 5 for 9; Perrin, 3 for 8.
PASSING
Dallas—Staubach, 17 of 25 for 183, 1 TD; Newhouse, 1 of 1 for 29, 1 TD; D. White, 1 of 2 for 5.
Denver—Morton, 4 of 15 for 39, 4 int.; Weese, 4 of 10 for 22.
RECEIVING
Dallas—P. Pearson, 5 for 37; DuPree, 4 for 66; Newhouse, 3 for -1; Johnson, 2 for 53, 1 TD; Richards, 2 for 38, 1 TD; Dorsett, 2 for 11; D. Pearson, 1 for 13.
Denver—Dolbin, 2 for 24; Odoms, 2 for 9; Moses, 1 for 21; Upchurch, 1 for 9; Jensen, 1 for 5; Perrin, 1 for -7.
PUNTING
Dallas—D. White, 5 for 208, 41.6 average.
Denver—Dilts, 4 for 153, 38.2 average.
PUNT RETURNS
Dallas—Hill, 1 for 1.
Denver—Upchurch, 3 for 22; Schultz, 1 for 0.
KICKOFF RETURNS
Dallas—Johnson, 2 for 29; Brinson, 1 for 22.
Denver—Upchurch, 3 for 94; Schultz, 2 for 62; Jensen, 1 for 17.
INTERCEPTIONS
Dallas—Washington, 1 for 27; Kyle, 1 for 19; Barnes, 1 for 0; Hughes, 1 for 0.
Denver—None.

Super Bowl XIII
Pittsburgh 35, Dallas 31

The NFL owners had changed the rules of pro football, making it easier to protect the passer and allowing receivers to move into the secondary without being bounced around like bumper pool balls. Most teams had approached the changes gingerly. In this rematch of Game X, Pittsburgh would exploit them fully.

Pittsburgh quarterback Terry Bradshaw started by connecting with John Stallworth for a 28-yard touchdown. Before he was finished he threw three more scoring aerials, including a record-tying 75-yarder, and had amassed 318 yards passing.

When linebacker Thomas (Hollywood) Henderson roughed him after a whistle blew, Franco Harris become enraged. Bradshaw immediately sent Harris up the middle against a blitz for a 22-yard scoring run. "Franco ran as hard as I've ever seen him run," said Bradshaw.

But the Cowboys were not exactly wallflowers. They answered the Steelers' first score with one of their own—a 39-yard pass to Tony Hill. Dallas went ahead in the second quarter when blitzing linebacker Mike Hegman stripped the ball from Bradshaw's hands and bolted 37 yards for a touchdown. But on a pivotal play in the third quarter, with Pittsburgh leading 21-14, Dallas tight end Jackie Smith dropped a sure touchdown pass in the end zone, and the Cowboys had to settle for a field goal.

It was close right to the end, with Dallas scoring on Roger Staubach's second and third touchdown passes within a little more than two minutes as the fourth quarter wound down.

Both touchdown drives were sandwiched around a successful onside kick.

The first drive ended with a eight-yard scoring pass to tight end Billy Joe DuPree. The second drive followed the onside kick. With 26 seconds left in the game, wide receiver Butch Johnson caught a four-yard touchdown pass.

Dallas tried another onside kick, but it was recovered by Rocky Bleier to end the game.

"Bradshaw was the difference," said Dallas safety Charlie Waters.

"He can throw a ball twenty yards," added Cliff Harris, "like I can throw a dart twenty feet."

Participants—Pittsburgh Steelers, champions of the American Football Conference, and Dallas Cowboys, champions of the National Football Conference
Date—January 21, 1979
Site—Orange Bowl, Miami
Time—4:15 P.M. EST
Conditions—71 degrees, cloudy
Playing surface—Grass
Television—National Broadcasting Company (NBC)
Radio—Columbia Broadcasting System (CBS)
Regular Season Records—Pittsburgh, 14-2, Dallas, 12-4
Conference Championships—Pittsburgh defeated the Houston Oilers 34-5 for the AFC title; Dallas defeated the Los Angeles Rams 28-0 for the NFC title
Players' Shares—$18,000 to each member of the winning team; $9,000 to each member of the losing team
Attendance—79,484
Gross Receipts—$8,833,185.26
Officials—Referee, Pat Haggerty; umpire, Art Demmas; line judge, Jack Fette; head linesman, Jerry Bergman; back judge, Pat Knight; side judge, Dean Look; field judge, Fred Swearingen
Coaches—Chuck Noll, Pittsburgh; Tom Landry, Dallas

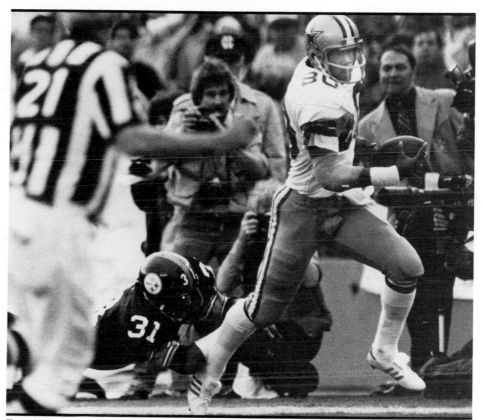

Tony Hill's 39-yard touchdown catch and run tied one of the most explosive Super Bowls.

Pittsburgh	Starters, Offense	Dallas
John Stallworth	WR	Tony Hill
Jon Kolb	LT	Pat Donovan
Sam Davis	LG	Herbert Scott
Mike Webster	C	John Fitzgerald
Gerry Mullins	RG	Tom Rafferty
Ray Pinney	RT	Rayfield Wright
Randy Grossman	TE	Billy Joe DuPree
Lynn Swann	WR	Drew Pearson
Terry Bradshaw	QB	Roger Staubach
Rocky Bleier	RB	Robert Newhouse
Franco Harris	RB	Tony Dorsett
	Starters, Defense	
L. C. Greenwood	LE	Ed Jones
Joe Greene	LT	Larry Cole
Steve Furness	RT	Randy White
John Banaszak	RE	Harvey Martin
Jack Ham	LLB	Thomas Henderson
Jack Lambert	MLB	Bob Breunig
Loren Toews	RLB	D. D. Lewis
Ron Johnson	LCB	Benny Barnes
Mel Blount	RCB	Aaron Kyle
Donnie Shell	LS	Charlie Waters
Mike Wagner	RS	Cliff Harris

Pittsburgh	7	14	0	14	—	35
Dallas	7	7	3	14	—	31

Pitt —Stallworth 28 pass from Bradshaw (Gerela kick)
Dall—Hill 39 pass from Staubach (Septien kick)
Dall—Hegman 37 fumble recovery return (Septien kick)
Pitt —Stallworth 75 pass from Bradshaw (Gerela kick)
Pitt —Bleier 7 pass from Bradshaw (Gerela kick)
Dall—FG Septien 27
Pitt —Harris 22 run (Gerela kick)
Pitt —Swann 18 pass from Bradshaw (Gerela kick)
Dall—DuPree 7 pass from Staubach (Septien kick)
Dall—Johnson 4 pass from Staubach (Septien kick)

TEAM STATISTICS

	Pitt	Dall
First downs	19	21
Rushing	2	6
Passing	15	13
By penalty	2	2
Total yardage	357	330
Net rushing yardage	66	154
Net passing yardage	291	176
Passes att.-comp.-had int.	30-17 1	30-17-1

RUSHING
Pittsburgh—Harris, 20 for 68, 1 TD; Bleier, 2 for 3; Bradshaw, 2 for -5.
Dallas—Dorsett, 16 for 96; Staubach, 4 for 37; Laidlaw, 3 for 12; P. Pearson, 1 for 6; Newhouse, 8 for 3.

PASSING
Pittsburgh—Bradshaw, 17 of 30 for 318, 4 TDs, 1 int.
Dallas—Staubach, 17 of 30 for 228, 3 TDs, 1 int.

RECEIVING
Pittsburgh—Swann, 7 for 124, 1 TD; Stallworth, 3 for 115, 2 TDs; Grossman, 3 for 29; Bell, 2 for 21; Harris, 1 for 22; Bleier, 1 for 7, 1 TD.
Dallas—Dorsett, 5 for 44; D. Pearson, 4 for 73; Hill, 2 for 49, 1 TD; Johnson, 2 for 30, 1 TD; DuPree, 2 for 17, 1 TD; P. Pearson, 2 for 15.

PUNTING
Pittsburgh—Colquitt, 3 for 129, 43.0 average.
Dallas—D. White, 5 for 198, 39.6 average.

PUNT RETURNS
Pittsburgh—Bell, 4 for 27.
Dallas—Johnson, 2 for 33.

KICKOFF RETURNS
Pittsburgh—L. Anderson, 3 for 45.
Dallas—Johnson, 3 for 63; Brinson, 2 for 41; R. White, 1 for 0.

INTERCEPTIONS
Pittsburgh—Blount, 1 for 13.
Dallas—Lewis, 1 for 21.

Super Bowl XIV

Pittsburgh 31, Los Angeles 19

The Los Angeles Rams had come into the game with the poorest record ever for a Super Bowl participant: 9-7. Cynics had a field day.

The oddsmakers made them 11-point underdogs to the mighty Steelers, who had made the Super Bowl their personal festival. Not since Game IV, when Kansas City was considered 13 points inferior to Minnesota, had there been such a disparity.

But the Steelers—along with everyone else—got more than they expected.

At the end of the third quarter, the Rams led 19-17. Their defense had done something only Dallas (in Game XIII) had been able to do to the Steelers' running game: stop it. Unfortunately for Los Angeles, it couldn't shut off the passing game as well.

Early in the fourth quarter, Pittsburgh was confronted with a third and eight on its 27. Two receivers, the gifted Lynn Swann and Theo Bell, already had been forced out of the game.

Terry Bradshaw sent wide receiver John Stallworth deep downfield. Rod Perry had inside coverage on him. Dave Elmendorf had outside coverage.

Bradshaw's pass dropped in perfectly.

The play covered 73 yards for a touchdown to put the Steelers ahead 24-19.

The Rams came right back, driving to the Steelers' 32. Quarterback Vince Ferragamo went back to pass on first down, but didn't see middle linebacker Jack Lambert, who had dropped deep. Lambert sprang in front of intended receiver Ron Smith and intercepted on the 14 to shut off the Rams' threat.

Bradshaw then completed another pass, for 45 yards, to Stallworth. Five plays later, Franco Harris cracked over from the 1 for the deciding points.

The final score, 31-19, was deceiving, though. The Rams had made it one of the most exciting Super Bowls games of all; the lead changed hands six times.

But in the end, it was the Steelers celebrating yet another great moment, a fourth Super Bowl victory.

"This was an invitation engraved in gold," said Joe Greene. "An invitation to immortality."

Participants—Pittsburgh Steelers, champions of the American Football Conference, and the Los Angeles Rams, champions of the National Football Conference
Date—January 20, 1980
Site—Rose Bowl, Pasadena
Time—3:15 P.M. PST
Conditions—67 degrees, sunny
Playing surface—Grass
Television and Radio—Columbia Broadcasting System (CBS)
Regular Season Records—Pittsburgh, 12-4; Los Angeles 9-7
Conference Championships—Pittsburgh defeated the Houston Oilers 27-13 for the AFC title; Los Angeles defeated the Tampa Bay Buccaneers 9-0 for the NFC title
Players' Shares—$18,000 to each member of the winning team; $9,000 to each member of the losing team
Attendance—103,985
Gross Receipts—$9,489,274.00
Officials—Referee, Fred Silva; umpire, Al Conway; line judge, Bob Beeks; head linesman, Burl Toler; back judge, Stan Javie; side judge, Ben Tompkins; field judge, Charley Musser
Coaches—Chuck Noll, Pittsburgh; Ray Malavasi, Los Angeles

The lead changed hands six times, and almost seven, until Jack Lambert's late interception.

Los Angeles	Starters, Offense	Pittsburgh
Billy Waddy	WR	John Stallworth
Doug France	LT	Jon Kolb
Kent Hill	LG	Sam Davis
Rich Saul	C	Mike Webster
Dennis Harrah	RG	Gerry Mullins
Jackie Slater	RT	Larry Brown
Terry Nelson	TE	Bennie Cunningham
Preston Dennard	WR	Lynn Swann
Vince Ferragamo	QB	Terry Bradshaw
Cullen Bryant	RB	Rocky Bleier
Wendell Tyler	RB	Franco Harris
	Starters, Defense	
Jack Youngblood	LE	L. C. Greenwood
Mike Fanning	LT	Joe Greene
Larry Brooks	RT	Gary Dunn
Fred Dryer	RE	John Banaszak
Jim Youngblood	LLB	Dennis Winston
Jack Reynolds	MLB	Jack Lambert
Bob Brudzinski	RLB	Robin Cole
Pat Thomas	LCB	Ron Johnson
Rod Perry	RCB	Mel Blount
Dave Elmendorf	LS	Donnie Shell
Nolan Cromwell	RS	J. T. Thomas

Los Angeles	7	6	6	0 —	19
Pittsburgh	3	7	7	14 —	31

Pitt—FG Bahr 41
LA —Bryant 1 run (Corral kick)
Pitt—Harris 1 run (Bahr kick)
LA —FG Corral 31
LA —FG Corral 45
Pitt—Swann 47 pass from Bradshaw (Bahr kick)
LA —R. Smith 24 pass from McCutcheon (kick failed)
Pitt—Stallworth 73 pass from Bradshaw (Bahr kick)
Pitt—Harris 1 run (Bahr kick)

TEAM STATISTICS	LA	Pitt
First downs	16	19
Rushing	6	8
Passing	9	10
By penalty	1	1
Total yardage	301	393
Net rushing yardage	107	84
Net passing yardage	194	309
Passes att.-comp.-had int.	26-16-1	21-14-3

RUSHING

Los Angeles—Tyler, 17 for 60; Bryant, 6 for 30, 1 TD; McCutcheon, 5 for 10; Ferragamo, 1 for 7.
Pittsburgh—Harris, 20 for 46, 2 TDs; Bleier, 10 for 25; Bradshaw, 3 for 9; Thornton, 4 for 4.

PASSING

Los Angeles—Ferragamo, 15 of 25 for 212, 1 int.; McCutcheon, 1 of 1 for 24, 1 TD.
Pittsburgh—Bradshaw, 14 of 21 for 309, 2 TDs, 3 int.

RECEIVING

Los Angeles—Waddy, 3 for 75; Bryant, 3 for 21; Tyler, 3 for 20; Dennard, 2 for 32; Nelson, 2 for 20; D. Hill, 1 for 28; Smith, 1 for 24, 1 TD; McCutcheon, 1 for 16.
Pittsburgh—Swann, 5 for 79, 1 TD; Stallworth, 3 for 121, 1 TD; Harris, 3 for 66; Cunningham, 2 for 21; Thornton, 1 for 22.

PUNTING

Los Angeles—Clark, 5 for 220, 44.0 average.
Pittsburgh—Colquitt, 2 for 85, 42.5 average.

PUNT RETURNS

Los Angeles—Brown, 1 for 4.
Pittsburgh—Bell, 2 for 17; Smith, 2 for 14.

KICKOFF RETURNS

Los Angeles—E. Hill, 3 for 47; Jodat, 2 for 32; Andrews, 1 for 0.
Pittsburgh—L. Anderson, 5 for 162.

INTERCEPTIONS

Los Angeles—Elmendorf, 1 for 10; Brown, 1 for 6; Perry, 1 for -1; Thomas, 0 for 6.
Pittsburgh—Lambert, 1 for 16.

Super Bowl XV

Oakland 27, Philadelphia 10

The matchup between Oakland and Philadelphia could have been an anti-climax. The teams had met earlier in the regular season and the Eagles won 10-7 in a primitive, hard-hitting game.

The score was less important than what the Eagles' defense had done to Oakland's passing game. The aging Raiders' offensive linemen could not protect Cinderella quarterback Jim Plunkett. The Eagles sacked him eight times, three by Claude Humphrey.

Evidence that the Super Bowl game would be different came when Ron Jaworski threw his first pass of the game and linebacker Rod Martin intercepted it.

Oakland moved to the Eagles' 2-yard line. The Philadelphia pass rushers went after Plunkett, but he scrambled deftly out of trouble, passing to Cliff Branch in the end zone for the Raiders' first touchdown.

In the final minute of the first quarter, the Eagles forced Plunkett from the pocket again. On the run, he spotted Kenny King at the Raiders' 39 and passed to him. King ran the rest of the way to the end zone untouched for the longest touchdown play in Super Bowl history, 80 yards.

Philadelphia kicker Tony Franklin came through on a 30-yard field goal in the second quarter, but the quarter ended on a block of his 28-yard attempt by freelancing Raiders linebacker Ted Hendricks. The score was 14-3; the Raiders were rolling.

By the third quarter, the Raiders' linemen were totally dominating the Eagles' pass rushers, giving Plunkett ease and comfort. He threw 32 yards to Bob Chandler and then 29 yards to Branch, who seemed covered perfectly by rookie Roynell Young, but then took position and made a leaping reception for a touchdown.

Philadelphia gamely pushed to the Raiders' 34, then Martin made the second of his record three interceptions. Chris Bahr's subsequent field goal made it 24-3 and the Raiders were on their way to becoming the first wild card team to win the Super Bowl.

Participants—Oakland Raiders, champions of the American Football Conference, and Philadelphia Eagles, champions of the National Football Conference
Date—January 25, 1981
Site—Louisiana Superdome, New Orleans
Time—5:15 P.M. CST
Conditions—72 degrees, indoors
Playing surface—AstroTurf
Television—National Broadcasting Company (NBC)
Radio—Columbia Broadcasting System (CBS)
Regular Season Records—Oakland, 11-5; Philadelphia, 12-4
Conference Championships—Oakland defeated the San Diego Chargers 34-27 for the AFC title; Philadelphia defeated the Dallas Cowboys 20-7 for the NFC title
Players' Shares—$18,000 to each member of the winning team; $9,000 to each member of the losing team
Attendance—76,135
Gross Receipts—$10,328,664.57
Officials—Referee, Ben Dreith; umpire, Frank Sinkovitz; line judge, Tom Dooley; head linesman, Tony Veteri; back judge, Tom Kelleher; side judge, Dean Look; field judge, Fritz Graf
Coaches—Tom Flores, Oakland; Dick Vermeil, Philadelphia

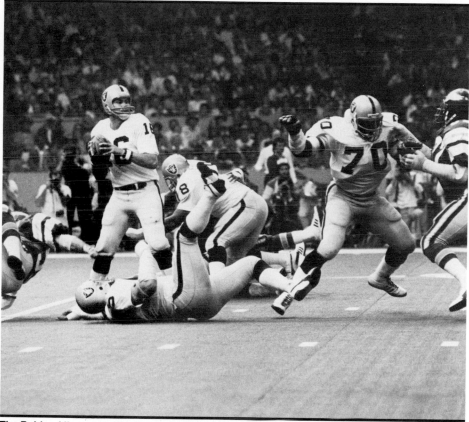

The Raiders' line gave Jim Plunkett all day to throw, and he gave them a Super Bowl victory.

Oakland	Starters, Offense	Philadelphia
Clifford Branch	WR	Harold Carmichael
Art Shell	LT	Stan Walters
Gene Upshaw	LG	Petey Perot
Dave Dalby	C	Guy Morriss
Mickey Marvin	RG	Woody Peoples
Henry Lawrence	RT	Jerry Sisemore
Raymond Chester	TE	Keith Krepfle
Bob Chandler	WR-TE	John Spagnola
Jim Plunkett	QB	Ron Jaworski
Mark van Eeghen	RB	Leroy Harris
Kenny King	RB	Wilbert Montgomery
	Starters, Defense	
John Matuszak	LE	Dennis Harrison
Reggie Kinlaw	NT	Charlie Johnson
Dave Browning	RE	Carl Hairston
Ted Hendricks	LOLB	John Bunting
Matt Millen	LILB	Bill Bergey
Bob Nelson	RILB	Frank LeMaster
Rod Martin	ROLB	Jerry Robinson
Lester Hayes	LCB	Roynell Young
Dwayne O'Steen	RCB	Herman Edwards
Mike Davis	LS	Randy Logan
Burgess Owens	RS	Brenard Wilson

Oakland	14	0	10	3	— 27
Philadelphia	0	3	0	7	— 10

Oak—Branch 2 pass from Plunkett (Bahr kick)
Oak—King 80 pass from Plunkett (Bahr kick)
Phil—FG Franklin 30
Oak—Branch 29 pass from Plunkett (Bahr kick)
Phil—Krepfle 8 pass from Jaworski (Franklin kick)
Oak—FG Bahr 35

TEAM STATISTICS	Oak	Phil
First downs	17	19
Rushing	6	3
Passing	10	14
By penalty	1	2
Total yardage	377	360
Net rushing yardage	117	69
Net passing yardage	260	291
Passes att.-comp.-had int.	21-13-0	38-18-3

RUSHING
Oakland—van Eeghen, 19 for 80; King, 6 for 18; Jensen, 3 for 12; Plunkett, 3 for 9; Whittington, 3 for -2.
Philadelphia—Montgomery, 16 for 44; Harris, 7 for 14; Giammona, 1 for 7; Harrington, 1 for 4; Jaworski, 1 for 0.
PASSING
Oakland—Plunkett, 13 of 21 for 261, 3 TDs.
Philadelphia—Jaworski, 18 of 38 for 291, 1 TD, 3 int.
RECEIVING
Oakland—Branch, 5 for 67, 2 TDs; Chandler, 4 for 77; King, 2 for 93, 1 TD; Chester, 2 for 24.
Philadelphia—Montgomery, 6 for 91; Carmichael, 5 for 83; Smith, 2 for 59; Krepfle, 2 for 16, 1 TD; Spagnola, 1 for 22; Parker, 1 for 19; Harris, 1 for 1.
PUNTING
Oakland—Guy, 3 for 126, 42.0 average.
Philadelphia—Runager, 3 for 110, 36.7 average.
PUNT RETURNS
Oakland—Matthews, 2 for 1.
Philadelphia—Sciarra, 2 for 18; Henry, 1 for 2.
KICKOFF RETURNS
Oakland—Matthews, 2 for 29; Moody, 1 for 19.
Philadelphia—Campfield, 5 for 87; Harrington, 1 for 0.
INTERCEPTIONS
Oakland—Martin, 3 for 44.
Philadelphia—None.

Super Bowl XVI

San Francisco 26, Cincinnati 21

Game XVI was the first northern Super Bowl, played in the Pontiac Silverdome, some 40 miles north of frigid, snow-covered Detroit in the midst of the worst winter in memory. The action inside the dome, though, was hot right from the start. San Francisco 49ers rookie Amos Lawrence fumbled the opening kickoff and the Cincinnati Bengals recovered at the 49ers' 26. But, six plays later, the momentum reversed as 49ers safety Dwight Hicks intercepted Ken Anderson's pass at the San Francisco 5 and returned it 27 yards. From there, quarterback Joe Montana drove the 49ers to the Bengals' 1, where he took the ball in himself on a sneak.

Another turnover cued the 49ers' second touchdown. Eric Wright, one of three rookies starting in the 49ers' secondary, stripped the ball from Cris Collinsworth after the Bengals' rookie wide receiver had made a 19-yard reception. Then *another* rookie, cornerback Lynn Thomas, recovered at the 49ers' 8. Montana, the game's most valuable player, made the most of the turnover with the longest touchdown drive in Super Bowl history, 92 yards.

The 49ers padded their lead with 15 seconds remaining in the first half with a 22-yard field goal by Ray Wersching. Wersching's ensuing kickoff, a bounding squibber (the kind that gave the Bengals fits all day), was fumbled by Archie Griffin and the 49ers recovered at the 4 with five seconds left. A 26-yard field goal made the halftime score 20-0, the largest Super Bowl half-time deficit ever.

Anderson came out firing in the second half, engineering an 83-yard scoring drive capped by his own five-yard run. Later in the third period, after a 49-yard reception by Collinsworth, the Bengals had a first-and-goal at the 3. With one of the great Super Bowl defensive efforts (including a third-down, one-on-one goal-line tackle of running back Charles Alexander by linebacker Dan Bunz), the 49ers held.

The Bengals managed to draw within six points (20-14) early in the fourth quarter, but Wersching's third and fourth field goals of the game (tying a Super Bowl record) put it out of reach.

Participants—Cincinnati Bengals, champions of the American Football Conference, and San Francisco 49ers, champions of the National Football Conference
Date—January 24, 1982
Site—Pontiac Silverdome, Pontiac
Time—4:00 P.M. EST
Conditions—70 degrees, indoors
Playing Surface—AstroTurf
Television and Radio—Columbia Broadcasting System (CBS)
Regular Season Records—Cincinnati, 12-4; San Francisco, 13-3
Conference Championships—Cincinnati defeated the San Diego Chargers 27-7 for the AFC title; San Francisco defeated the Dallas Cowboys 28-27 for the NFC title
Players' Shares—$18,000 to each member of the winning team; $9,000 to each member of the losing team
Attendance—81,270
Gross Receipts—$10,641,034.83
Officials—Referee, Pat Haggerty; umpire, Al Conway; line judge, Bob Beeks; head linesman, Jerry Bergman; back judge, Bill Swanson; side judge, Bob Rice; field judge, Don Hakes
Coaches—Forrest Gregg, Cincinnati; Bill Walsh, San Francisco

Dwight Hicks's interception ended the Bengals' first drive and led to the 49ers' first score.

San Francisco	Starters, Offense	Cincinnati
Dwight Clark	WR	Cris Collinsworth
Dan Audick	LT	Anthony Munoz
John Ayers	LG	Dave Lapham
Fred Quillan	C	Blair Bush
Randy Cross	RG	Max Montoya
Keith Fahnhorst	RT	Mike Wilson
Charle Young	TE	Dan Ross
Freddie Solomon	WR	Isaac Curtis
Joe Montana	QB	Ken Anderson
Ricky Patton	RB	Pete Johnson
Earl Cooper	RB	Charles Alexander
	Starters, Defense	
Jim Stuckey	LE	Eddie Edwards
Archie Reese	NT	Wilson Whitley
Dwaine Board	RE	Ross Browner
Willie Harper	LOLB	Bo Harris
Jack Reynolds	LILB	Jim LeClair
Craig Puki	RILB	Glenn Cameron
Keena Turner	ROLB	Reggie Williams
Ronnie Lott	LCB	Louis Breeden
Eric Wright	RCB	Ken Riley
Carlton Williamson	LS	Bobby Kemp
Dwight Hicks	RS	Bryan Hicks

San Francisco	7	13	0	6	—	26
Cincinnati	0	0	7	14	—	21

SF —Montana 1 run (Wersching kick)
SF —Cooper 11 pass from Montana (Wersching kick)
SF —FG Wersching 22
SF —FG Wersching 26
Cin—Anderson 5 run (Breech kick)
Cin—Ross 4 pass from Anderson (Breech kick)
SF —FG Wersching 40
SF —FG Wersching 23
Cin—Ross 3 pass from Anderson (Breech kick)

TEAM STATISTICS	SF	Cin
First downs	20	24
Rushing	9	7
Passing	9	13
By penalty	2	4
Total yardage	275	356
Net rushing yardage	127	72
Net passing yardage	148	284
Passes att.-comp.-had int.	22-14-0	34-25-2

RUSHING
San Francisco—Patton, 17 for 55; Cooper, 9 for 34; Montana, 6 for 18, 1 TD; Ring, 5 for 17; Davis, 2 for 5; Clark, 1 for -2.
Cincinnati—Johnson, 14 for 36; Alexander, 5 for 17; Anderson, 4 for 15, 1 TD; A. Griffin, 1 for 4.

PASSING
San Francisco—Montana, 14 of 22 for 157, 1 TD.
Cincinnati—Anderson, 25 of 34 for 300, 2 TDs, 2 int.

RECEIVING
San Francisco—Solomon, 4 for 52; Clark, 4 for 45; Cooper, 2 for 15, 1 TD; Wilson, 1 for 22; Young, 1 for 14; Patton, 1 for 6; Ring, 1 for 3.
Cincinnati—Ross, 11 for 104, 2 TDs; Collinsworth, 5 for 107; Curtis, 3 for 42; Kreider, 2 for 36; Johnson, 2 for 8; Alexander, 2 for 3.

PUNTING
San Francisco—Miller, 4 for 185, 46.3 average.
Cincinnati—McInally, 3 for 131, 43.7 average.

PUNT RETURNS
San Francisco—Hicks, 1 for 6.
Cincinnati—Fuller, 4 for 35.

KICKOFF RETURNS
San Francisco—Hicks, 1 for 23; Lawrence, 1 for 17; Clark, 1 for 0.
Cincinnati—Verser, 5 for 52; A. Griffin, 1 for 0; Frazier, 1 for 0.

INTERCEPTIONS
San Francisco—Hicks, 1 for 27; Wright, 1 for 25.
Cincinnati—None.

Super Bowl XVII
Washington 27, Miami 17

Super Bowl XVII was the Hogs (the Washington Redskins' huge offensive line plus the man they opened holes for, honorary hog John Riggins) versus the Killer Bees (the Miami Dolphins' swarming defense, so named because so many of the starters' last names began with "B") in a 10-year anniversary rematch of Super Bowl VII.

Miami got an early score on a 76-yard pass from David Woodley to wide-open Jimmy Cefalo. Then, after trading second-quarter field goals, the Redskins tied the game on Joe Theismann's four-yard lob to Alvin Garrett.

Fulton Walker took the ensuing kickoff and did what he threatened to do on his previous 42-yard return—he took it all the way, 98 yards for the longest kickoff return in Super Bowl history and the first one for a score (1 of 11 individual and 13 team records set in the game).

Despite being on the wrong end of the 17-10 halftime score, Washington head coach Joe Gibbs had "a good feeling" about the second half that proved precognizant. The Redskins' defense came out and totally shut down the Dolphins; neither Woodley nor backup Don Strock completed a pass in the second half.

Even the Redskins *offense* contributed defensively. Shortly before the end of the third quarter, with Miami leading 17-13, Theismann went back to pass from his own 18. The pass he threw was tipped back at him by defensive end Kim Bokamper. As the pass hung in the air, Bokamper, on the dead run toward the Washington goal line, reached for it, but Theismann lunged and knocked the ball away.

The Dolphins weakened; Riggins (who gained a record 166 yards on 38 carries) seemed to get stronger. His 43-yard early fourth-quarter touchdown run, the longest scoring run from scrimmage in a Super Bowl, cemented the game's most valuable player award for him.

Theismann threw for one more fourth-quarter touchdown—six yards to Charlie Brown—to earn the team a 27-17 victory and a postgame congratulatory call phone from President Ronald Reagan. Still, Riggins had the last word. "At least for tonight," he said, "Ron may be the President, but I'm the king."

Participants—Miami Dolphins, champions of the American Football Conference, and Washington Redskins, champions of the National Football Conference
Date—January 30, 1983
Site—Rose Bowl, Pasadena
Time—3:00 P.M. PST
Conditions—61 degrees, clear
Playing Surface—Grass
Television—National Broadcasting Company (NBC)
Radio—Columbia Broadcasting System (CBS)
Regular Season Records—Miami, 7-2; Washington, 8-1
Conference Championships—Miami defeated the New York Jets 14-0 for the AFC title; Washington defeated the Dallas Cowboys 31-17 for the NFC title
Players' Shares—$36,000 to each member of the winning team; $18,000 to each member of the losing team
Attendance—103,667
Gross Receipts—$19,997,330.86
Officials—Referee, Jerry Markbreit; umpire, Art Demmas; line judge, Bill Reynolds; head linesman, Dale Hamer; back judge, Dick Hantak; field judge, Don Orr; side judge, Dave Parry
Coaches—Don Shula, Miami; Joe Gibbs, Washington

Quarterback Joe Theismann turned defender to break up Kim Bokamper's interception.

Miami	Starters, Offense	Washington
Duriel Harris	WR	Alvin Garrett
Jon Giesler	LT	Joe Jacoby
Bob Kuechenberg	LG	Russ Grimm
Dwight Stephenson	C	Jeff Bostic
Jeff Toews	RG	Fred Dean
Eric Laakso	RT	George Starke
Bruce Hardy	TE	Don Warren
Jimmy Cefalo	WR	Charlie Brown
David Woodley	QB	Joe Theismann
Tony Nathan	RB	John Riggins
Andra Franklin	RB-TE	Rick Walker
	Starters, Defense	
Doug Betters	LE	Mat Mendenhall
Bob Baumhower	NT-LT	Dave Butz
Kim Bokamper	RE-RT	Darryl Grant
Bob Brudzinski	LOLB-RE	Dexter Manley
A. J. Duhe	LILB-LLB	Mel Kaufman
Earnie Rhone	RILB-MLB	Neal Olkewicz
Larry Gordon	ROLB-RLB	Rich Milot
Gerald Small	LCB	Jeris White
Don McNeal	RCB	Vernon Dean
Glenn Blackwood	LS	Tony Peters
Lyle Blackwood	RS	Mark Murphy

Miami	7	10	0	0	—	17
Washington	0	10	3	14	—	27

Mia —Cefalo 76 pass from Woodley (von Schamann kick)
Wash—FG Moseley 31
Mia —FG von Schamann 20
Wash—Garrett 4 pass from Theismann (Moseley kick)
Mia —Walker 98 kickoff return (von Schamann kick)
Wash—FG Moseley 20
Wash—Riggins 43 run (Moseley kick)
Wash—Brown 6 pass from Theismann (Moseley kick)

TEAM STATISTICS	Mia	Wash
First downs	9	24
Rushing	7	14
Passing	2	9
By penalty	0	1
Total yardage	176	400
Net rushing yardage	96	276
Net passing yardage	80	124
Passes att.-comp.-had int.	17-4-1	23-15-2

RUSHING
Miami—Franklin, 16 for 49; Nathan, 7 for 26; Woodley, 4 for 16; Vigorito, 1 for 4; Harris, 1 for 1.
Washington—Riggins, 38 for 166, 1 TD; Garrett, 1 for 44; Harmon, 9 for 40; Theismann, 3 for 20; Walker, 1 for 6.
PASSING
Miami—Woodley, 4 of 14 for 97, 1 TD, 1 int.; Strock, 0 of 3 for 0.
Washington—Theismann, 15 of 23 for 143, 2 TD, 2 int.
RECEIVING
Miami—Cefalo, 2 for 82, 1 TD; Harris, 2 for 15.
Washington—Brown, 6 for 60, 1 TD; Warren, 5 for 28; Garrett, 2 for 13, 1 TD; Walker, 1 for 27; Riggins, 1 for 15.
PUNTING
Miami—Orosz, 6 for 227, 37.8 average.
Washington—Hayes, 4 for 168, 42.0 average.
PUNT RETURNS
Miami—Vigorito, 2 for 22.
Washington—Nelms 6 for 52.
KICKOFF RETURNS
Miami—Walker, 4 for 190, 1 TD; L. Blackwood, 2 for 32.
Washington—Nelms, 2 for 44; Wonsley, 1 for 13.
INTERCEPTIONS
Miami—Duhe, 1 for 0; L. Blackwood, 1 for 0.
Washington—Murphy, 1 for 0.

Captions and Credits

Credits
Editor **Jim Natal**
Photo Editor **David Boss**
Designer **Glen Iwasaki**

1. Morning at midfield, Super Sunday XVII. *Photo by Al Messerschmidt*
2. A Super Bowl record 103,438 fans perform an appearing act at Game XI in Pasadena's Rose Bowl. *Peter Read Miller*
4. The Vince Lombardi Trophy, symbol of the NFL championship. *Fred Anderson*
6. The shadows of a January afternoon transform the crowd arriving at the Louisiana Superdome for Game XV into a concourse of Giacometti sculptures. *Vernon J. Biever*
7. Looking like the inside of the mother ship in *Close Encounters of the Third Kind,* the Superdome looms above the action of Super Bowl XII. *Peter Read Miller*
8-9. The Super Bowl has become an international media event attracting a television audience of more than 100 million. *David Boss*
9. (Inset) A small army of technicians brandishing state-of-the-art equipment converge to telecast each Super Bowl game. *Michael Zagaris*
10. A participant in the "Caribbean Holiday" halftime spectacular at Super Bowl XIII. *Al Messerschmidt*
11. A montage of fans and celebrants at Super Bowls XIII and XV. *Ross Lewis*
(Bottom, left): Doc Severinsen, here, along with Al Hirt, played a sort of Super Bowl of trumpets at Game IV. *David Boss*
12. (Clockwise from top left): A relaxed ticket seeker at Game XIII *Ross Lewis*; Mardi Gras floats color halftime at Game XV *Malcolm Emmons*; Redskins fans at Game XVII perform their own halftime card stunt. *Al Messerschmidt*
13. A steam-spouting papier-maché giant at Super Bowl II towers over the Green Bay Packers as they prepare to take the field. *Malcolm Emmons*
14-15. Balloons, blimps, and Pasadena's San Gabriel mountains contribute to the pregame panorama at Game XVII. *Miguel Elliot*
15. (Inset) Pittsburgh's Roy Gerela tees up the ball to kick off the action at Super Bowl X. *John Biever*

Games
32. The fans in the stands help make the Super Bowl what it is. A total of 1,400,480 people have attended the 17 Super Bowl games held in seven different stadiums. *David Boss*
34-35. Behind the blocking of tackle Forrest Gregg (75), Jim Taylor sets up the final Packers touchdown on a run to the Chiefs' 1 yard line. Defensive tackle Andy Rice made the stop. *James Flores*
36. Wide receiver Max McGee, the unlikely hero of Game I for the Packers, shakes off cornerback Willie Mitchell en route to one of his two touchdowns. *Darryl Norenberg*
37. NFL Commissioner Pete Rozelle presents Green Bay head coach Vince Lombardi with the NFL World Championship Trophy at Game I. The sterling silver trophy was created by Tiffany and Company; a new one is presented each year to the winning team. *Vernon Biever*

38. Daryle Lamonica, the Raiders' "Mad Bomber," passed for 208 yards and two touchdowns—not enough, though, to beat the Packers. *Malcolm Emmons*
39. With surgical precision and superior line play, Bart Starr and the Packers probed the Raiders' defense in the air and on the ground; they gained 322 total yards in Super Bowl II. Starr received his second consecutive MVP award. *David Boss*
40. (Top left) Running back Tom Matte argues a call at Super Bowl III. *Darryl Norenberg*
(Top right) Running back Jerry Hill voices his displeasure at the course of the game. *David Boss*
(Bottom) Jets cornerback Randy Beverly (42) steals Johnny Unitas's end zone pass intended for Jimmy Orr (28) in the fourth quarter. It was the fourth Colts drive stopped by an interception, and the second by Beverly. *Malcolm Emmons*
41. Body language says it all for Colts tackle Bob Vogel late in the fourth quarter of Game III. *David Boss*
42. After guaranteeing victory for his New York Jets team in Super Bowl III, quarterback Joe Namath passed for 206 yards to help make his prophecy come true. *Malcolm Emmons*
43. Bill Mathis (31) leads the way as Matt Snell makes one of his 30 carries that were good for 121 total yards and one touchdown. *Vernon Biever*
44-45. Kansas City running back Mike Garrett cuts back against the grain and scores easily on a five-yard run in the second quarter. *Malcolm Emmons*
46-47. All eyes were on Chiefs quarterback Len Dawson at Super Bowl IV. The patches worn on the Chiefs' left shoulders were ordered for the game by Kansas City owner and AFL co-founder Lamar Hunt to commemorate the league's 10 seasons. *Vernon Biever*
47. At the Super Bowl, as at any game, the scoreboard has the last word. *Tony Tomsic*
48. Baltimore Colts kicker Jim O'Brien (80) and his holder, quarterback Earl Morrall, go airborne to signal that O'Brien's Game V-winning 32-yard field goal sailed true. *Malcolm Emmons*
49. (Top) Colts middle linebacker Mike Curtis (32) finds himself at the right place at the right time to intercept Craig Morton's sideline pass that popped out of the hands of leaping Dallas running back Dan Reeves. *David Boss*
(Bottom) With a tight grip on his facemask, Dallas cornerback Mel Renfro is lost in thought in the final seconds of Game V. *David Boss*
50. The confidence and versatility of Cowboys quarterback Roger Staubach made the difference for Dallas in Game VI. He ran for 18 yards and passed for 119 and two touchdowns to win most valuable player honors. *Malcolm Emmons*
51. (Top) Walt Garrison gained 74 yards in Game VI as Dallas overpowered Miami on the ground. *Vernon Biever*
(Bottom) Like all cowboys are supposed to do, head coach Tom Landry rides off into the Super Bowl VI sunset. *Tony Tomsic*
52. Late in the fourth quarter of Game VII, Dolphins safety Jake Scott (13) intercepted Billy Kilmer's pass intended for Charley Taylor in the end zone and returned it 55 yards, all but crushing Washington's chances for victory. *Nate Fine*

53. The Redskins' Larry Brown meets the immovable force, Dolphins tackle Manny Fernandez. *David Boss*
54-55. (Top, left) Miami kicker Garo Yepremian had to think fast on his feet when he recovered his field goal attempt blocked by Washington's Bill Brundige (77) in Game VII. *David Boss*
(Bottom, left) Yepremian's subsequent pass attempt went awry as well. *Tony Tomsic*
(Right) Mike Bass (41) turned the broken play into Washington's only score of the day, racing 49 yards down the sideline with 2:07 remaining. *Dick Raphael*
56. Vikings defensive tackle Alan Page pleads his case against a roughing the passer call to no avail in Game VIII. *David Boss*
57. Miami's Larry Csonka scores his second touchdown on a two-yard run in the third quarter. Vikings defenders Wally Hilgenberg and Bob Lurtsema (75) can only watch. *Bob Allen*
58. The Steelers' defense made sure Super Bowl IX was not Fran Tarkenton's day. The Minnesota quarterback was tackled in the end zone for a safety, had three passes intercepted, and four others knocked down. *Hitoshi Suzumori*
58-59. Super Sunday IX was a great day for Terry Bradshaw (12), who led Pittsburgh to its first NFL championship. *Malcolm Emmons*
59. Running back Franco Harris broke rushing records (34 carries for 158 yards and one touchdown) and Minnesota's spirits in Game IX. *Dick Raphael*
60. While players and officials trot upfield for the point after touchdown attempt, quarterback Terry Bradshaw, barely conscious, is helped off the field after being hit while passing for a score in the fourth quarter of Super Bowl X. *Herb Weitman*
61. On the play that Bradshaw went down, wide receiver Lynn Swann (88) went up for the 64-yard catch that won the game. Linebacker Jack Lambert hoists Swann for all to see. *John Iacono*
62. Dallas's Mark Washington gets a ringside seat for one of Lynn Swann's four acrobatic catches that gained 161 yards in Game X. *Heinz Kluetmeier*
63. Pittsburgh linebackers Andy Russell (34) and Jack Ham (59) bend to the task of bringing down the Cowboys' Preston Pearson. *Vernon Biever*
64. Tight end Dave Casper of Oakland keeps his eyes—and hands—on the ball long enough to score the first touchdown of Game XI, a one-yard pass from Ken Stabler in the second quarter. *Peter Read Miller*
65. (Top) To Oakland players buoyed by their Super Bowl XI victory over the Vikings, even head coach John Madden seems lighter than air. *John Biever*
(Bottom) With Minnesota's fourth Super Bowl loss confirmed, Vikings running back Chuck Foreman (44) holds back bitter tears from Charles Goodrum. *Fred Anderson*
66. Ballet turns into seven points as Dallas wide receiver Butch Johnson performs a *pas de trois* with Denver defenders Bernard Jackson (29) and Steve Foley at Super Bowl XII. *The Allens Studio*
67. Thinking the roof of the Superdome must have collapsed on him, Broncos quarterback Craig Morton topples under the Cowboys' Ed (Too Tall) Jones. *Vernon Biever*

68. The Steelers' offensive line didn't have a nick-name, but it was made of metal strong enough to protect Terry Bradshaw in Game XII. *Manny Rubio*

69. (Top) As Dallas defensive end Ed (Too Tall) Jones set his sights on quarterback Terry Bradshaw, running back Rocky Bleier sets his on Jones. *Dave Cross*
(Bottom) Wide receiver John Stallworth (82) tied Game XIII in the second quarter by carrying a reception 75 yards for a touchdown. Mike Hegman (58) and Cliff Harris pursued to no avail. *Dave Cross*

70. Cowboys tight end Jackie Smith can't believe he dropped the pass that would have tied Game XIII going into the fourth quarter. *Malcolm Emmons*

71. (Sequence) With or without the assist from the official, Pittsburgh's Franco Harris was a man intent on getting into the end zone on this 22-yard run early in the fourth quarter. *Al Messerschmidt*

72. Wendell Tyler (26) had to leave Game XIV five times, but the doughty Rams running back came back to take, as well as give, more. *Vernon Biever*

72-73. Though it looks like a kung fu move by Los Angeles safety Dave Elmendorf (42), Steelers running back Rocky Bleier shows a few moves of his own in Game XIV. *Dave Cross*

73. Pittsburgh middle linebacker Jack Lambert makes like the comic book man of steel in an unsuccessful attempt to break up Lawrence McCutcheon's 24-yard scoring option pass to Ron Smith. *Dave Cross*

74-75. (Sequence) Terry Bradshaw and John Stallworth connected for a 73-yard touchdown in Game XIV on a play that hadn't worked all week in practice. *Amos Love*

76. Philadelphia quarterback Ron Jaworski got racked, sacked, and outright attacked by the Raiders' rush in Super Bowl XV. *Dave Cross*

76-77. Oakland's Cliff Branch rises from the end zone after catching Jim Plunkett's 29-yard touchdown pass in the third quarter of Game XV. *Dave Cross*

77. Oakland linebacker Ted Hendricks blocks Tony Franklin's second quarter 28-yard field goal attempt to deprive the Eagles of one of their few scoring opportunities in Super Bowl XV. *Dave Cross*

78. (Top) Cincinnati tight end Dan Ross celebrates the first of his two fourth-quarter touchdown catches, which combined with his nine other receptions, set a Super Bowl record. *Tony Tomsic*
(Bottom) Quarterback Joe Montana, in only his third year with the 49ers (and his first as a full-time starter), led the team to its first NFL championship. *John Biever*

79. The 49ers' defense punctuates its goal-line stand that helped stem the Bengals' tide in the second half of Game XVI. *Manny Rubio*

80. (Top) Tony Peters (23) was the only man to beat and Miami wide receiver Jimmy Cefalo beat him for the opening touchdown of Game XVII. *Peter Read Miller*
(Bottom) On his record 98-yard touchdown return, Fulton Walker outraced the entire Redskins kick-off team. *Richard Mackson*

81. Washington fans go hog wild as John Riggins goes 43 yards for a score. *Diane Kaluza*

Players and Coaches

82. San Francisco defenders contemplate what awaits them outside the locker room. *Michael Zagaris*

84. Green Bay Packers head coach Vince Lombardi at Super Bowl II: a larger than life man at a larger than life game. *Malcolm Emmons*

85. Bart Starr's success in Game I was built on the blocking of his line, including guard Fuzzy Thurston (63) and tackle Forrest Gregg (75). *James Flores*

86. Defensive tackle Buck Buchanan of the Chiefs comes in for a rough landing in Game I. The landing was even rougher for Packers quarterback Bart Starr. *Tony Tomsic*

87. Oakland running back Hewritt Dixon tries to elude pursuing defensive end and team co-captain Willie Davis of Green Bay in Game II. *Malcolm Emmons*

88. Audacious quarterback Joe Namath (12) kept the Jets' confidence high for Game III. *Darryl Norenberg*

89. Baltimore running back Tom Matte gained 116 of the Colts' 143 rushing yards in Super Bowl III, including a record run of 58 yards from scrimmage. *Darryl Norenberg*

90. In Super Bowl IV, Len Dawson called the shots for the Chiefs. *Tony Tomsic*

91. Super Bowl V quarterback Earl Morrall of Baltimore hands off to running back Norm Bulaich (36) as Tom Nowatzke (34) leads the way past crashing Dallas defensive tackle Bob Lilly (74). The play set up Baltimore's final touchdown late in the fourth quarter. *Dick Raphael*

92. Cowboys running back Duane Thomas, silent most of the year, did his talking with his rushing at Game VI. He gained 95 yards and scored one touchdown. *John Biever*

93. Dolphins quarterback Bob Griese is tackled for a 29-yard loss by Dallas's Bob Lilly at Super Bowl VI. *Manny Rubio*

94. Miami defensive tackle Manny Fernandez was in control in Game VII. *Tony Tomsic*

95. Larry Brown was the main man in Washington's running game on the way to, and at, Super Bowl VII. *Malcolm Emmons*

96. Seemingly impervious to Vikings tacklers Paul Krause (22) and Jeff Siemon, Dolphins running back Larry Csonka thunders to his first touchdown 10 plays into Super Bowl VIII. *Malcolm Emmons*

97. (Top) Minnesota quarterback Fran Tarkenton runs from the Steelers' rush in Game IX. *Malcolm Emmons*
(Right) Head coach Bud Grant makes his point from the sideline. *David Boss*
(Bottom) Steelers linebacker Jack Lambert separates wide receiver John Gilliam from the ball. *Manny Rubio*

98. Pittsburgh defensive tackle Mean Joe Greene dispenses a mean look. *Bill Amatucci*

99. Jack Lambert takes a rest while the Steelers' offense goes to work. *R.H. Stagg*

100. The Oakland Raiders' offensive line forms a pocket around the Super Bowl XI Trophy. *Dennis Desprois*

101. Three quarters of the air wing of the Raiders' offense at Game XI: quarterback Ken Stabler (12), and wide receivers Cliff Branch (21) and Fred Biletnikoff (25). *Peter Read Miller*

102. Denver's swarming Orange Crush defense, led by end Lyle Alzado (77) and linebackers Randy Gradishar (53) and Bob Swenson (51), held Dallas superstar running back Tony Dorsett to 66 yards rushing in Game XII, but couldn't hold the Cowboys out of the end zone. *Peter Read Miller*

103. Tom Landry, the only head coach the Dallas Cowboys have ever had, reflects on his second Super Bowl triumph after Game XII. *Peter Read Miller*

104-105. The doomsday duo of Dallas's Doomsday II defense, Randy White (54) and Harvey Martin (79), were in a jocular mood after Game XII. *John Biever*

105. Benched late in Super Bowl XII, Broncos quarterback Craig Morton sits deep in thought as the game goes by. Morton began his professional career with the Cowboys, leading them on the field at Game V. *Peter Read Miller*

106. The Rams' defense, emotionally charged by its leader, defensive end Jack Youngblood, held the Steelers to but 84 yards rushing in Game XIV. In this action, Larry Brooks (90), Mike Fanning (79), and Youngblood (85) stop Rocky Bleier. *Malcolm Emmons*

107. (Top) John Stallworth came into his own against the Rams. *Darryl Norenberg*
(Bottom) Steelers quarterback Terry Bradshaw got tougher as Game XIV did. *John Biever*

108. Rags-to-riches Oakland quarterback Jim Plunkett is embraced by ecstatic safety Burgess Owens after Super Bowl XV. *Michael Zagaris*

109. While Raiders head coach Tom Flores holds up one finger to indicate his first Super Bowl victory, linebacker Rod Martin (53) could hold up two more than that, one for each of his record three Game XV interceptions. *Michael Zagaris*

110. Behind center Blair Bush's block on Dwaine Board, Cincinnati quarterback Ken Anderson scrambles to find a receiver in Super Bowl XVI. *Al Messerschmidt*

111. (Sequence, top and center) As running back Charles Alexander catches a third-down swing pass, 49ers linebacker Dan Bunz catches him and stops him in his tracks at the 1 yard line. *Vernon Biever*
(Sequence, bottom) Alexander is left to wonder who, or what, hit him as side judge Bob Rice signals fourth down. *Tony Tomsic*

112. San Francisco linebacker Jack Reynolds goes over defensive strategy in the locker room. *Michael Zagaris*

113. As if viewing the shades of his three past Super Bowls, Miami guard Bob Kuechenberg stands transfixed at Game XVII. *George Gojkovich*

114-115. Washington running back John Riggins is caught in a rare moment of repose at Super Bowl XVII. *Al Messerschmidt*

Sidelines

116. The finger of fate points Washington's way at Game XVII. *Manny Rubio*

118-119. Halftime at Super Bowl XIV was an explosion of color and Big Band sound created by Up With People. *Herb Weitman*

119. (Inset) Chicago Bears owner (and one of the

NFL's founders) George Halas was the honored guest at Game XIII, there to flip the coin prior to kickoff. *Manny Rubio*

120. An 80-foot wide yellow ribbon marks the Louisiana Superdome at Super Bowl XV, commemorating the release of the American hostages who had been held in Iran. *Ross Lewis*

121. Raiders cheerleaders strut the Superdome sideline at Game XV. *Al Messerschmidt*

122-123. The Apollo 16 space capsule, back from the moon, was on display at Super Bowl VII, accompanied by its crew, Charles Duke, Ken Mattingly, and John Young. *David Boss*

123. (Inset) Lunar orbiting Apollo 8 astronauts Jim Lovell, Frank Borman, and Bill Anders lead the Super Bowl III crowd in the Pledge of Allegiance. *David Boss*

124-125. The Goodyear Blimp slides in low over the Orange Bowl in Miami at Super Bowl X as part of the filming of the movie *Black Sunday*. *David Boss*

124. (Inset, left) *Black Sunday* star, the late Robert Shaw (left), and director John Frankenheimer take five on the Orange Bowl bench. *Tony Tomsic* (Inset, right) The film crew sets up a shot. *The Academy Foundation*

125. (Inset, left) Robert Shaw runs an end zone route. *The Academy Foundation*
(Inset, right) Extras scatter for cover as the blimp's game ends. *The Academy Foundation*

126-127. The best vantage point for Game XVII's 12-minute-long card flashing extravaganza was from the air. *Baron Wolman*

127. (Inset) Diana Ross added some Motown magic to the National Anthem at Game XVI in the Pontiac Silverdome. *Al Messerschmidt*

128. A hot air balloon, part of Super Bowl IV's planned pregame entertainment, makes an unplanned landing in the end zone. *Vernon Biever*

129. She looks inflatable, but the Bourbon Street stripper was practicing her "art" for real in frigid Tulane Stadium at Game IX. *Carl Skalak, Jr.*

130-131. Steelers faithful unfurl an enormous "Terrible Towel," Pittsburgh's whammy-inducing charm, at Game XIV. *George Long*

130. (Inset) The 1979 World Series most valuable player, Pittsburgh's Willie Stargell, greets Steelers quarterback and Super Bowl XIII and XIV most valuable player, Terry Bradshaw. *Michael Zagaris*

132. (Inset) The members of the Super Bowl Press Club, who had covered every Super Bowl to date, convened at Game XV with NFL Commissioner Pete Rozelle. They are (standing, left to right) Edwin Pope, Larry Felser, Cooper Rollow, Mel Durslag, Jerry Green, Tony Tomsic, Mickey Palmer, Jerry Izenberg, Dave Klein, Robert Burnes, John Seguin, Will McDonough, Vernon Biever, Dick Connor, and Bob Oates. Seated: Jim Murray, Norm Miller, John Steadman, Bud Lea, Rozelle, Augie Lio, Gene Roswell, Dave Brady, and Si Burick. *Ross Lewis*

132-133. NFL Commissioner Pete Rozelle meets the press prior to Game XV. *Ross Lewis*

134-135. The Caribbean-flavored halftime show at Game XIII sets Miami's Orange Bowl aglow. An enormous custom-made Caribbean map carpet was unrolled, performed upon, rolled up, and removed in 20 minutes' time. *Ross Lewis*

Emotions

136. Marauding Oakland linebacker Ted Hendricks signals victory at Super Bowl XV. *Bill Smith*

138. Cornerback Fred Williamson was the Chiefs' main mouthpiece before Game I. *Vernon Biever*

138-139. Green Bay guard Fuzzy Thurston (63) congratulates running back Elijah Pitts (22) on his five-yard touchdown run early in the third quarter, giving the Packers a 21-10 lead. *David Boss*

140. Gleeful head coach Weeb Ewbank is surrounded by his New York Jets players, Dave Herman (67), Mark Smolinski (30), and Matt Snell (41), at the conclusion of Super Bowl III. *Fred Roe*

141. A Colts player gets a helping hand in putting the Game III loss in perspective. *Ross Lewis*

142-143. A fallen Viking, quarterback Joe Kapp, grimaces in pain late in the fourth quarter of Game IV. *Dick Raphael*

143. Kansas City wide receiver Otis Taylor is greeted heartily by running back Mike Garrett upon returning from a trip to the end zone in Game IV. *Darryl Norenberg*

144-145. Chiefs head coach Hank Stram samples life at the top after winning Super Bowl IV. *Rod Hanna*

146. (Inset) With the stadium crowd on its feet, Baltimore kicker Jim O'Brien winds up to deliver the kick that won Game V. *Dick Raphael*

146-147. As the Colts get set to launch a postgame celebration, Dallas's Bob Lilly launches his helmet in frustration. *Manny Rubio*

148-149. Dallas defenders George Andrie and Jethro Pugh stand in a neutral corner as Colts quarterback Johnny Unitas stays down for the count. *Russ Russell*

149. Exuberant Colts assistant coach John Sandusky pounds Dallas's despondent Dan Reeves (30) as he shoves past Mike Curtis (32), who intercepted a ball off Reeves's hands late in Game V. Earl Morrall (15) and Tom Nowatzke (34) help make Reeves feel worse. *David Boss*

150. Redskins star running back Larry Brown sees his Super Bowl VII victory hopes vanishing. *Dick Raphael*

151. The end of a perfect season at Super Bowl VII was the beginning of an era for Miami head coach Don Shula. *Vernon Biever*

152-153. After Game VIII, Dolphins coach Don Shula catches his choked-up defensive assistant, Bill Arnsparger, who was moving on to the New York Giants as head coach the next season. *John Walther*

154. The entire Pittsburgh defense, including Dwight White (78), Ernie Holmes (63), and Jack Lambert (58) had hands in defeating the Vikings in Game IX. *Tony Tomsic*

155. Steelers linebacker Jack Lambert stands ready to deny another inch to Dallas running back Robert Newhouse in Game X. *Vernon Biever*

156. Flanked by linebacker Ted Hendricks, Oakland's Willie Hall (39) holds aloft the ball he recovered to stop a Vikings' drive near the goal line at Game XI. Minnesota quarterback Fran Tarkenton turns his attention inward. *Fred Anderson*

157. Looking like Atlas in football pads holding up the Superdome roof, Dallas defensive end Harvey Martin signals victory. *John Biever*

158. Denver wide receiver-kick returner Rick Upchurch

searches for solace as Game XII slips away. *The Allens Studio*

159. Rams running back Lawrence McCutcheon signals the result as teammate Cullen Bryant (32) scores in the first quarter of Super Bowl XIV. *Michael Zagaris*

160. The Steelers and Rams both sense, in their respective ways, that Game XIV is over after Franco Harris (32) ran for a late one-yard touchdown. *Manny Rubio*

161. Satisfaction doesn't come easily to Pittsburgh head coach Chuck Noll—unless it comes in the form of a Super Bowl Trophy. *Michael Zagaris*

162. Philadelphia's Claude Humphrey throws a flag himself after being flagged for roughing the passer in Game XV. *Richard Mackson*

162-163. Amid postgame bedlam, disappointed Eagles head coach Dick Vermeil (center right) gives Oakland's Cinderella quarterback, Jim Plunkett, a pat on the shoulder as photographers swarm the field. *Herb Weitman*

164. Rookie linebacker Matt Millen (55) and nose tackle Reggie Kinlaw share their elation over winning the Super Bowl. *Dave Cross*

165. The expression on the face of Eagles rookie cornerback Roynell Young is as telling as the scoreboard. *David Boss*

166-167. San Francisco nose tackle Archie Reese (78) plays king of the mountain after helping stop the Bengals on fourth down at the goal line. *Tony Tomsic*

168. Rookie 49ers cornerback Eric Wright tries to rearrange rookie wide receiver Cris Collinsworth's Bengal stripes after a 49-yard reception in Game XVI. *David Boss*

169. San Francisco guard Randy Cross (51) and nose tackle Archie Reese react to the halftime gun of Game XVI as the 49ers leave the field with a 20-0 lead. *David Boss*

170. The Redskins' circus, featuring wide receivers Alvin Garrett (89) and leaping Charlie Brown (87), and running back Clarence Harmon (38), performs in the Rose Bowl end zone after scoring the final touchdown of Game XVII. *Al Messerschmidt*

171. It's all in a day's work for John Riggins, the picture of nonchalance after shouldering the rushing load for Washington in Super Bowl XVII. *Richard Mackson*

Appendix

173. *Vernon Biever*
174. *Vernon Biever*
175. *Vernon Biever*
176. *Malcolm Emmons*
177. *Wide World Photos*
178. *David Boss*
179. *Jay Spencer*
180. *David Boss*
181. *Pittsburgh Steelers*
182. *Malcolm Emmons*
183. *Peter Read Miller*
184. *Peter Read Miller*
185. *Dave Cross*
186. *Vernon Biever*
187. *David Boss*
188. *Dave Cross*
189. *Rob Brown*